Essential Business Grammar Builder

Scan the CD at the back of the book

Macmillan Education
Between Towns Road, Oxford OX4 3PP
A division of Macmillan Publishers Limited
Companies and representatives throughout the world

ISBN 978-1-4050-7046-1

First published 2006

Original design by Mike Brain Graphic Design Limited, Oxford
Page make-up by Anthony Godber
Illustrated by Karen Donnelly
Cover design by Jackie Hill at 320 Design
Cover photograph by Getty Images

The author would like to thank David Riley for commissioning the book and providing his usual
exemplary input to both the details and the big picture, Karen Spiller for her careful and creative
editing and Jill Leatherbarrow for her thorough work on the index (again).

The authors and publishers would like to thank the following for permission to reproduce their cartoons:
Cartoonbank pp10 @The New Yorker Collection 1986 Lee Lorenz from cartoonbank.com. All Rights Reserved.,
12 @The New Yorker Collection 2000 J.B. Handelsman from cartoonbank.com. All Rights Reserved.,
19 @The New Yorker Collection 2003 Peter Steiner from cartoonbank.com. All Rights Reserved.,
20 @The New Yorker Collection 1997 Sidney Harris from cartoonbank.com. All Rights Reserved.,
22 @The New Yorker Collection 1982 Bud Grace from cartoonbank.com. All Rights Reserved.,
32 @The New Yorker Collection 2000 P.C.Vey from cartoonbank.com. All Rights Reserved.,
38 @The New Yorker Collection 1995 Robert Mankoff from cartoonbank.com. All Rights Reserved.,
42 @The New Yorker Collection 2004 Sam Gross from cartoonbank.com. All Rights Reserved.,
47 @The New Yorker Collection 2004 Glen Lelievre from cartoonbank.com. All Rights Reserved.,
54 @The New Yorker Collection 1975 Dana Fradon from cartoonbank.com. All Rights Reserved.,
56 @The New Yorker Collection 1997 Leo Cullum from cartoonbank.com. All Rights Reserved.,
58 @The New Yorker Collection 1987 Dean Victor from cartoonbank.com. All Rights Reserved.,
87 @The New Yorker Collection 2002 Sidney Harris from cartoonbank.com. All Rights Reserved.,
94 @The New Yorker Collection 1986 Robert Weber from cartoonbank.com. All Rights Reserved.,
100 @The New Yorker Collection 1985 Michael Maslin from cartoonbank.com. All Rights Reserved.,
106 @The New Yorker Collection 1995 J.B. Handelsman from cartoonbank.com. All Rights Reserved.,
112 @The New Yorker Collection 1988 Charles Barsotti from cartoonbank.com. All Rights Reserved.,
116 @The New Yorker Collection 1987 Leo Cullum from cartoonbank.com. All Rights Reserved.,
120 @The New Yorker Collection 2005 Peter Steiner from cartoonbank.com. All Rights Reserved.,
123 @The New Yorker Collection 1991 Robert Weber from cartoonbank.com. All Rights Reserved.
www.CartoonStock.com pp34, 37, 64, 66, 78, 91, 102, 122, 126

Printed in Thailand

2014 2013 2012
10 9 8 7 6

Essential

Paul Emmerson

Business
Grammar
Builder

MACMILLAN

Contents

CONTENTS

Test bank

Appendices

Answer key

Index

Grammar terms and test

Active form	form of the verb when the person or thing doing the action is the subject of the verb: *I **wrote** the report.* (See 'Passive form'.)
Adjective	describes a noun: *quick, large, international*
Adverb	describes a verb: *quickly, yesterday, in France*
Affirmative	sentence that is not a negative or question
Article	words *the* (= definite article) or *a/an* (= indefinite article)
Auxiliary verb	verb used before other verbs to make questions, negative sentences, tenses, passives, etc. Auxillary verbs are: *be, do, have* and modal verbs
Clause	group of words that contains a subject and a verb
Comparative	form of an adjective used when comparing two things: *Google is **more popular** than Yahoo.*
Conditional	clause beginning with a word like *if, unless* which says what must happen in order for the information in the other part of the sentence to be true
Consonant	any letter of the alphabet except *a, e, i, o, u*
Continuous form	form of the verb that ends in *-ing* and shows an action in progress
Contraction	short form of a word that is made by leaving out letters: ***I'll*** = *I will*
Determiner	word that goes before a noun and identifies (*the, my*) or quantifies (*some, many*)
Imperative	base form of the verb that expresses a command: ***Come** here. **Switch** it off.*
Infinitive	base form of the verb, used with or without *to: come, to come, work, to work*
***-ing* form**	form of the verb that ends in *-ing: going, making, marketing*
Intransitive verb	verb that does not take an object: *arrive, happen, sleep, wait, work*
Irregular	form that does not follow a rule: *go – went – gone, man – men, bad – worse*
Linking word	word that joins two clauses (*and, but, so*) or makes a connection between two sentences (*furthermore, however, therefore*)
Modal verb	*can, could, will, would, must, may, might, shall, should*
Negative	sentence made with *not* (*n't*): *He **doesn't work** in the sales department.*
Noun	name of an object, idea, place or person: *car, freedom, Italy, Susan*
Object	person or thing affected by a verb: *I've read **the report**.*
Passive form	form of the verb when the subject (person or thing) is affected by the action of the verb: *The report **was written** by me.* (See 'Active form'.)
Past participle	form of the verb used in perfect tenses and passives; you can find it in the third column of verb tables: *worked, gone, seen*
Phrasal verb	verb + preposition that gives a new meaning: *deal with, take off, wake up*
Plural	form that refers to two or more people or things: *cars, people*
Possessive	form that shows who or what something belongs to: *my, mine, Jane's*
Preposition	word like *at, behind, in, through, with* that shows place, movement, time, etc
Pronoun	word like *it, me, you, myself, someone* that takes the place of a noun
Reflexive pronoun	word like *myself, ourselves* that is used when the person who does the action is also affected by it
Relative clause	clause beginning with *who, which, that,* etc that identifies or describes
Reported speech	also called *indirect speech* – when we report what someone said without using their exact words: *'I**'ll** be **there**.'* → *She said she**'d** be **here**.*
Simple	form of the verb that does not use an auxiliary verb: *I **agree**, she **agreed***
Singular	form that refers to one person or thing
Subject	person or thing that does the action of the verb: ***Peter** works here.*
Superlative	form of an adjective used when comparing one thing with all the others: *Microsoft Office is **the most popular** computer software.*
Transitive verb	verb that is followed by an object: *buy, discuss, manufacture, want*
Verb	word that expresses an action or state: *arrive, know*
Vowel	letters *a, e, i, o, u*

Test

1 Match examples a)–p) with grammar terms 1–16 below.

a) *a/an, the*

b) *at, to, for*

c) *do, have*

d) *can, must, might*

e) *If you do that, I'll ...*

f) *she, someone, myself*

g) *happy, important, good*

h) *slowly, carefully, well*

i) *all, some, both, either*

j) *product, computer, information, advice*

k) *but, however, because, for example, in fact*

l) *worked, seen, lived, known*

m) <u>get up</u> *in the morning,* <u>deal with</u> *a problem*

n) *The letter* <u>that arrived this morning</u> *is for you.*

o) *The company* <u>was founded</u> *in 1995.*

p) *'I'll call you.'* → *He said he'd call me.*

1	linking words	k	7	pronouns	☐	13	conditional sentence	☐
2	auxiliary verbs	☐	8	articles	☐	14	relative clause	☐
3	modal verbs	☐	9	adjectives	☐	15	reported speech	☐
4	phrasal verbs	☐	10	adverbs	☐	16	past participles	☐
5	prepositions	☐	11	determiners	☐			
6	nouns	☐	12	passive form	☐			

2 Match verb forms a)–h) with their names 1–8 below.

a) Helen *is arriving* in Prague tomorrow afternoon.

b) I*'ve been working* here for two years.

c) I *saw* Toshiro yesterday – he sends his regards.

d) I usually *leave* home at about 7.30 and *get* to work an hour later.

e) I*'m going to visit* Madrid next month. I hope *we'll have* a chance to meet.

f) By the time we got to the station, the train *had left*.

g) I*'ve lived* in Athens all my life.

h) While I *was giving* my presentation, someone at the back interrupted me.

1	present simple	d	5	past simple	☐
2	present continuous	☐	6	past continuous	☐
3	present perfect	☐	7	past perfect	☐
4	present perfect continuous	☐	8	future forms	☐

To the student: learning grammar and speaking English

To improve your spoken English you have to go through several stages. A grammar book will help you on your way.

1 **Awareness** You see where the problems are for the first time.

2 **Passive understanding** You can do the exercises, but can't produce the grammar in speech. You recognize situations where you need the grammar to express yourself.

3 **Production, with mistakes** You try to use the grammar in speech, but make mistakes. If someone points out a mistake, or you notice it yourself, you can self-correct.

4 **Reasonably accurate and fluent speech** at intermediate level. Congratulations!

1 Present simple

A Form

This table shows the present simple of the verb *to work*.

Affirmative	Negative	Question
I work	*I do not (don't) work*	*Do I work?*
You work	*You do not (don't) work*	*Do you work?*
He/she/it works	*He/she/it does not (doesn't) work*	*Does he/she/it work?*
We work	*We do not (don't) work*	*Do we work?*
They work	*They do not (don't) work*	*Do they work?*

- (NOT ~~He work in a bank.~~)
- (NOT ~~He doesn't to work in a bank.~~)
- (NOT ~~He doesn't works in a bank.~~)
- We use contractions (in brackets) in speech and informal writing.

"We study, we plan, we research. And yet, somehow, money still remains more of an art than a science."

B Uses

- We use the present simple for permanent situations.
  *Nike **manufactures** sportswear.*
- We use the present simple for regular routines.
  *It often **takes** an hour to answer all my emails.*
- We use the present simple for habits.
  *I **go** to Austria every winter to do some skiing.*
- We use the present simple for scientific and other facts.
  *Stainless steel **contains** chromium.*
- In general, we use the present simple to describe actions and situations that are always or generally true.

C Time adverbs

- To talk about routines and habits we can use frequency adverbs: *always, often, usually, sometimes, occasionally, rarely, never.*

  Note the positions.
  Before the main verb: *The Swiss franc **usually rises** at times of international crisis.*
  After the verb *be*: *Czech beer **is usually** very good.*

- Other frequency adverbs include: *every day/week/month, daily/weekly/monthly, once a day/four times a year, from time to time, most of the time,* etc.

  These can come at the beginning or end of the sentence.
  ***Four times a year** we **prepare** a sales report.*
  *We **prepare** a sales report **four times a year**.*

  We use the present simple to refer to the future after these words: *after, as soon as, before, if, in case, unless, until, when.*
  *Be ready **in case** he **calls** you.*
  ***When** the parcel **arrives**, let me know.*

Exercises

1.1 <u>Underline</u> the correct words.

1 Violet *work/works* at our Head Office in Paris now.

2 Violet *doesn't to work/doesn't work* in Spain any more.

3 Our company *produce/produces* parts for the automobile industry.

4 Our company *doesn't have/doesn't has* a factory in Europe.

5 Where *does you/do you* live?

6 Where *does he/do he* live?

7 Increased competition *often causes/causes often* a fall in prices.

8 Increased competition *always is/is always* bad for profits.

9 I'll let you know as soon as *I hear/I'll hear* from him.

10 When *you'll get back/you get back* from Madrid, send me an email.

1.2 Complete the article about Wal-Mart by using these verbs in the present simple: *close, ~~dominate~~, employ, open, not/pay, rule.*

Walmart number 1 in retailing

Wal-Mart is the biggest corporation in the world. It (1) _dominates_ retailing in the US, with sales of more than $250 billion a year, and it (2) _____ three times more people than General Motors. Of the ten richest people in the world, five are Waltons – the family which (3) _____ the Wal-Mart empire. But the success of Wal-Mart has its controversial side. Wal-Mart (4) _____ very good salaries, and when a big store (5) _____ in an out-of-town location, the local shops often (6) _____ .

1.3 Complete the dialogue by putting the verbs into the present simple.

HELMUT: It's a good conference, isn't it?

TATIANA: Yes, it is. (1) _____ (you/come) every year?

HELMUT: Not every year. It (2) _____ (depend) on whether I have the time. I (3) _____ (work) in technical support in the IT area and we often have to deal with a crisis at short notice. We (4) _____ (not/know) our job schedule from one week to the next. But I (5) _____ (come) to the conference whenever I can. What about you? What (6) _____ (you/do)?

TATIANA: I'm an information systems manager. I (7) _____ (direct) the work of systems analysts, computer programmers and support specialists like you. Listen, can I ask you something? (8) _____ (you/plan) to stay in your company for ever?

HELMUT: Well, I like my work, but of course if someone (9) _____ (make) me a more attractive offer, I'll consider it. Why? What (10) _____ (you/have) in mind?

TATIANA: Our company often (11) _____ (need) IT technicians, and we pay well. Here's my card. Give me a call next week. We (12) _____ (not/have) any vacancies at the moment, but we're a big organization and we may be recruiting more people soon.

2 Present continuous

"I'm not trying to sell you anything, sir. I'm doing market research, and all I ask is two or three hours of your time to answer a few thousand questions."

Last month David Noble was appointed chairman of Pyaterochka, a Russian supermarket group. 'The country **is growing** dynamically and consumers **are getting** wealthier. Unless you want to give up working and live on a beach, this is the most exciting place to be,' Noble says.

Telegraph website

A trial **is currently taking place** at the High Court which raises questions about accountancy firms and the way in which they are insured.

Accountancy Age website

A Form

● We form the present continuous with the auxiliary verb *be* and the *-ing* form of the verb.

Affirmative	Negative	Question
I am ('m) working	*I am not ('m not) working*	*Am I working?*
You are ('re) working	*You are not (aren't) working*	*Are you working?*
He/she/it is ('s) working	*He/she/it is not (isn't) working*	*Is he/she/it working?*
We are ('re) working	*We are not (aren't) working*	*Are we working?*
They are ('re) working	*They are not (aren't) working*	*Are they working?*

● We use contractions (in brackets) in speech and informal writing.

● The negative has an alternative form: *you're not, he/she/it's not, we're not, they're not.*

● If a verb ends with the letter *-e*, we leave it out when we add *-ing*. So we write: *we are having* (NOT ~~haveing~~), *they are coming* (NOT ~~comeing~~), etc.

● Some verbs are not normally used in a continuous form. (See unit 3.)

B Uses

● We use the present continuous to describe activities in progress right now, at the moment of speaking.

*Angela **is talking** to a client at the moment.*
*The network **isn't working** – the IT department **are trying** to remove a virus.*

● We use the present continuous to describe activities in progress now, but not at this exact moment.

*I'm **reading** a book about the life story of Bill Gates.*
*We're **negotiating** with the trade union. The next meeting is on Monday.*

● We use the present continuous to describe trends and developments in progress over a longer time period.

*The problem of global warming **is getting** worse.*
*Turkey **is developing** its links with the EU and the standard of living **is improving**.*

● In general, the present continuous describes an activity that is temporary rather than permanent. It has the idea of something happening for a limited time.

C Time adverbs

● We use the following time adverbs with the present continuous: *at present, at the moment, currently, now, nowadays, right now, these days, this week.*

*Our Public Relations department **is currently sponsoring** a range of sports events.*
***These days** more and more companies **are moving** production to South East Asia.*
***This week** I'm **taking** the bus to work – they're **repairing** my car at the garage.*

Exercises

2.1 Match the present continuous forms 1–3 with their uses a)–c) below.

1 Great conference! And I'm *staying* at the Sheraton, only five minutes away. ☐

2 More and more people *are using* the Internet to make telephone calls. ☐

3 I'm *calling* about our order number K356. ☐

a) something happening right at this moment

b) something happening around now, but not at this exact moment

c) a long-term trend/development

2.2 Underline the correct words.

1 *I writing/I'm writing* the report this week – it will be ready on Friday.

2 Mr Sorensen is busy at the moment. *He is expecting/Is he expecting* you?

3 The lift *isn't working/doesn't working*. We'll have to take the stairs.

2.3 Complete this article by using these verbs in the present continuous: become, *continue, co-operate, move.*

Japan and China: the connections get stronger

The economies of South East Asia (1) _are becoming_ more and more connected. Panasonic, a Japanese company, (2) _____ production of low-end products like televisions from Japan to China. At the same time it (3) _____ to manufacture high-end products, like industrial robots, in Japan. But many of these robots are then sold to Chinese companies. So Panasonic benefits from access to China in both cases. China and Japan have been rivals in the past, but these days they (4) _____ more and more. Who knows? One day there may even be a common currency: the Asian dollar.

2.4 Complete the conversation by putting the verbs into the present continuous.

FRANK: Hello, Jackie, what (1) _____ *are you doing* _____ (you/do) here in Hamburg?

JACKIE: I (2) _____ (visit) someone at Axel Springer, the publisher. We (3) _____ (develop) a project together to share digital media content.

FRANK: That sounds interesting. Where (4) _____ (you/stay)?

JACKIE: At the Crowne Plaza. And what about you? How (5) _____ (business/go)?

FRANK: As you know, the advertising industry (6) _____ (not/do) very well at the moment. Luckily our agency is OK, but the market (7) _____ (become) very fragmented – digital TV channels, films, specialist magazines, Internet sites. A lot of advertisements (8) _____ (not/reach) the target audience like they used to, and our clients know it.

JACKIE: I can see the problem, but I'm sure you'll be OK in the long term. After all, business can't survive without advertising.

Present simple and present continuous

A Present simple or continuous?

● Here is a summary of units 1 and 2:

Present simple	Present continuous
- permanent situations I **work** for a Russian oil company.	- temporary situations I'm **working** from home today.
- habits and routines We **have** a meeting every Monday.	- current activity, in progress now Ana is busy right now – she's **having** a meeting.
- facts that don't change We all **get** old one day.	- developments and trends The population of Japan **is getting** older.

● Remember that the time adverb often controls the tense.

Present simple adverbs include: *usually, every week, most of the time*, etc.

Present continuous adverbs include: *at the moment, currently, right now*, etc.

See units 1 and 2 for a more complete list.

B State verbs

● There are a number of verbs that describe states. A 'state' is a condition, not an action.
State verbs are not normally used in a continuous form.

I know what you mean.	(NOT ~~I am knowing what you are meaning.~~)
I don't understand.	(NOT ~~I'm not understanding.~~)

● State verbs include:

thinking	*agree, believe, imagine, know, realize, remember, think, understand*
the senses	*hear, smell, see, taste*
feelings / needs	*appreciate, hate, like, love, need, prefer, want, wish*
possession	*belong to, contain, have, own, possess*
appearance	*appear, look like, seem*
being	*be, exist*
others	*cost, depend, involve, matter, mean, measure, owe, weigh*

● A few state verbs can have both an 'action' meaning (where a continuous form is possible) and a 'state' meaning (where it is not). Examples include: *be, have, think.*

Our suppliers **are being** very difficult at the moment.	(action)
Our suppliers **are** Italian.	(state, so NOT ~~are being Italian~~)
I'm **having** problems with the computer.	(action)
I **have** two sisters.	(state, so NOT ~~I'm having two sisters.~~)
I'm **thinking** about changing my job.	(action)
I **think** there's a post office on the next street.	(state, so NOT ~~I'm thinking there's a post office~~)

Exercises

3.1 Put each verb into the present simple or present continuous.

1 We _____*are spending*_____ (spend) a lot of money on advertising this year.

2 Every year we _____*spend*_____ (spend) over €500,000 on raw materials.

3 I _____ (enjoy) this conference – it's more interesting than last year.

4 I _____ (enjoy) a glass of wine occasionally, but I don't drink much.

5 Central banks always _____ (raise) interest rates when inflation goes up.

6 The Federal Reserve _____ (raise) rates quite slowly at the moment.

7 The sales report is my responsibility. Most of the time I _____ (write) it.

8 This time Wu _____ (write) the sales report – I'm away on holiday.

9 Look! They _____ (sell) their new cell phone with a 10% discount!

10 Of course, in the winter we _____ (sell) more coats, hats and scarves.

11 She's Czech – she _____ (come) from Prague.

12 She _____ (come) from Prague, so she may be late.

3.2 Write ✓ if the sentence is possible, write ✗ if it is impossible.

1 I'm drinking white wine. ✓

2 I'm preferring white wine. ✗

3 That laptop belongs to me.

4 That laptop is belonging to me.

5 It's seeming complicated.

6 It's becoming complicated.

7 This machine is costing $1m.

8 This machine is working well.

9 I need your signature.

10 I am needing your signature.

11 We're giving a discount.

12 We're wanting a discount.

3.3 Put each verb in this email into the present simple or present continuous.

Subject comments on change of company name

Hello Viktor – how are you? Busy as always, I (1) _____ (imagine)! Thanks for your last email – I (2) _____ (agree) completely with your comments about the situation in the market. Currently we (3) _____ (make) a reasonable profit, but it may not last.

Actually, I (4) _____ (write) to you about something different. We (5) _____ (do) some market research at the moment – I (6) _____ (remember) that I mentioned it to you when we met last week. We (7) _____ (want) to find out what our customers think about our company name. We're probably going to change it. I've attached a document with some ideas – it won't take long to read. We (8) _____ (try) to find a name that is more modern and more European. Can you let me know what you think? I (9) _____ (need) your comments by the end of the month, if possible. I (10) _____ (appreciate) your help on this.

Thanks, Colleen.

Past simple

A Form

● This table shows the past simple of the verb *to work*.

Affirmative	Negative	Question
I worked	*I did not (didn't) work*	*Did I work?*
You worked	*You did not (didn't) work*	*Did you work?*
He/she/it worked	*He/she/it did not (didn't) work*	*Did he/she/it work?*
We worked	*We did not (didn't) work*	*Did we work?*
They worked	*They did not (didn't) work*	*Did they work?*

● The verb *to work* is regular. Regular verbs add *-d* or *-ed* to the infinitive to form the affirmative.

● For negatives and questions we use the auxiliary verb *did* and the infinitive (without *to*). (NOT ~~I didn't to work~~ or ~~Did you worked~~?)

● We use contractions (in brackets) in speech and informal writing.

B Irregular verbs

● There are many verbs where the affirmative of the past simple is irregular. There is a list on pages 150–1. Here are some common examples:

be – was/were	*come – came*	*grow – grew*	*meet – met*	*spend – spent*
become – became	*fall – fell*	*have – had*	*pay – paid*	*take – took*
begin – began	*feel – felt*	*know – knew*	*put – put*	*tell – told*
bring – brought	*get – got*	*leave – left*	*rise – rose*	*think – thought*
build – built	*give – gave*	*lose – lost*	*see – saw*	*win – won*
buy – bought	*go – went*	*make – made*	*sell – sold*	*write – wrote*

C Uses

● We use the past simple to talk about completed actions in the past.

*Philip Morris, the tobacco company, **changed** its name to Altria **in 2003**.*
*Pfizer, the world's largest drug company, **said yesterday** that fourth quarter earnings **rose**.*

● With the past simple we usually know when the action happened, and this may be mentioned or clear from the situation.

D Time adverbs

● With the past simple we use time adverbs like:

at	*at ten o'clock/at the end of the month/at the weekend*
in	*in the morning/in July/in 2001/in the 1980s/in the summer*
on	*on Tuesday/on Tuesday afternoon/on the tenth of March/on the 24th*
no preposition	*yesterday/a few days ago/last week/when I was young*

Exercises

4.1 Complete 1–3 using the past simple of these verbs: *be, give, go, have, know, survive*.
There is a mixture of affirmative, negative and question forms.

1 Enron ____*was*____ the biggest scandal in US financial history. They _____ from dominance of the US energy market in the 1990s to bankruptcy in 2001.

2 Investors at the time of Enron's collapse were shocked. They asked: _____ anyone at the top _____ what was happening? And _____ the auditors, investment bankers or analysts _____ any warnings?

3 When the authorities started to investigate Enron, there was a problem: they _____ _____ most of the important documents. The auditors, Arthur Andersen, had destroyed them. Arthur Andersen _____ _____ this scandal and closed down a few months later.

4.2 Cover the opposite page. Write down the past simple (affirmative form only) of the verbs in this list. Most, but not all, are irregular: *become, begin, build, buy, come, develop, get, give, go, grow, have, know, leave, make, meet, need, put, sell, take, think.*

4.3 Complete each sentence with a verb: *become, decide, finish, get, put, renovate* and a time adverb: *at, at, in, in, on, on.*

1 We _____*decided*_____ to have the conference call _____*on*_____ Friday morning.

2 I worked hard last year and I _____ a good bonus _____ December.

3 We _____ the meeting _____ seven o'clock in the evening.

4 They say they _____ the money in our account _____ the 21st.

5 We _____ the building _____ the beginning of the year.

6 Klaus Kleinfeld _____ chief executive of Siemens _____ 2005.

5 **4.4** Complete this article by putting the verbs into the past simple. Some are irregular.

Samsung: from dried fish to high tech

In 1938 Byung-Chull Lee (1) _____*started*_____ (start) a business in Korea called Samsung. He (2) _____ (sell) vegetables and dried fish to China. Ten years later he (3) _____ (have) his own manufacturing and sales operations, and the business (4) _____ (grow) quickly. Over the next few decades Samsung (5) _____ (buy) several insurance companies and department stores.

In the 1970s Samsung (6) _____ (invest) in heavy industries like chemicals and shipbuilding, but then in the 1980s they (7) _____ (begin) to focus more on technology and electronic products. In 1987 Kun-Hee Lee (8) _____ (take) the place of his father as Chairman of the company. In 1988 he (9) _____ (announce) the 'Second Foundation' of the company, directing Samsung towards becoming a world-class 21st century corporation.

5 Past continuous and *used to*

A Form

- We form the past continuous with *was/were* + the *-ing* form of the verb.

Affirmative	Negative	Question
I *was working*	I *was not (wasn't) working*	*Was* I *working?*
You *were working*	You *were not (weren't) working*	*Were* you *working?*
He/she/it *was working*	He/she/it *was not (wasn't) working*	*Was* he/she/it *working?*
We *were working*	We *were not (weren't) working*	*Were* we *working?*
They *were working*	They *were not (weren't) working*	*Were* they *working?*

- We use contractions (in brackets) in speech and informal writing.

B Uses

- We use the past continuous to talk about an activity in progress in the past.

  I *was living* abroad in 2004.
  I *was sitting* in Starbucks, checking my emails on my laptop.

- We often use the past continuous and past simple together. The past continuous gives the background situation, then the individual events are in the past simple.

  I *was working* for Airbus in Toulouse when I first *met* Jean-Claude.
  We *were waiting* in the departure lounge when Olga suddenly *appeared*.
  I *was writing* the report when the phone *rang*.

  We do not know from the past continuous verb form whether the action continued or not. Look at the third example. Perhaps I continued writing after the phone call, perhaps not.

C Time adverbs

- With the past continuous we often use *when* or *while*.

  I met Jean-Claude *when/while* I *was working* for Airbus.

D *Used to*

- *Used to* describes a long-term situation or repeated habit in the past. It suggests that the situation or habit is no longer true.

  I *used to* work in sales. (but now I don't)
  I *used to* play tennis. (but now I don't)

- Note that *used to* cannot describe a single event.

  We *launched* this line at the Paris Expo. (NOT ~~We used to launch~~)

- With negatives and questions *used to* becomes *use to*.

  Did you *use to* work in sales? I *didn't use to* work in sales.

Exercises

6

5.1 Complete the mini-dialogues by putting the verbs into the past continuous. Use contractions where possible.

1 A: Your meeting went on for a long time this morning.

   B: Yes, _____ *we were trying* _____ (we/try) to decide whether we need to cut the marketing budget.

2 A: Well, what do you think?

   B: Sorry, _____ (I/not/listen). Can you repeat what you said?

3 A: I called you several times yesterday afternoon, but I only got your voicemail.
   What _____ (you/do)?

   B: _____ (I/discuss) the strategic plan with Angela and Jaroslav.

4 A: I need to call the hospital. My son and his girlfriend had an accident in his car last night and
   _____ (they/not/wear) seat-belts. Luckily, _____
   (he/not/drive) very fast. It could have been much worse.

   B: Oh no, that's terrible!

5.2 In each sentence put one verb into the past simple and one into the past continuous.

1 When you ___*called*___ (call), I ___*was talking*___ (talk) to a client.

2 While I _____ (enter) some data into the spreadsheet, the computer _____ (crash).

3 Tim Berners-Lee _____ (invent) the World Wide Web in 1989, while he
   _____ (work) at CERN in Geneva.

4 I _____ (discover) some interesting information about their company, while I
   _____ (surf) the Internet.

5 Everyone _____ (wait) for the meeting to begin, when a message _____ (arrive)
   from Josef to say he was stuck in traffic.

6 The Leaning Tower of Pisa _____ (start) to lean in 1185, while they _____ (build) it.

5.3 Decide whether the underlined verb can also have the form *used to* + infinitive. If it can, write the alternative. If it cannot, write ~.

1 Before they built the motorway, it <u>took</u> me an hour to get to work.   *used to take*

2 I <u>saw</u> Slava last week – he sends his regards.   ~

3 In the old days we <u>had</u> many more meetings.

4 I <u>started</u> working at the bank when I was 21.

5 Eva <u>became</u> the office administrator after she
   had worked as Remy's secretary.

6 I <u>owned</u> a BMW, but now I own an Audi.

"Would you take the guy at Table 4? I used to be his broker."

19

6 Present perfect 1

A Form

- We form the present perfect with the auxiliary *has/have* + the past participle.

Affirmative	Negative	Question
I **have** ('**ve**) *worked*	I **have not** (**haven't**) *worked*	**Have** I *worked*?
You **have** ('**ve**) *worked*	You **have not** (**haven't**) *worked*	**Have** you *worked*?
He/she/it **has** ('**s**) *worked*	He/she/it **has not** (**hasn't**) *worked*	**Has** he/she/it *worked*?
We **have** ('**ve**) *worked*	We **have not** (**haven't**) *worked*	**Have** we *worked*?
They **have** ('**ve**) *worked*	They **have not** (**haven't**) *worked*	**Have** they *worked*?

- Regular verbs like *work* form the past participle with *-d* or *-ed*. In verb tables, the second column (past simple) and third column (past participle) are the same: *work – worked – worked*.

- Irregular verbs often have a different past simple and past participle: *do – did – **done**, go – went – **gone***. For a list of irregular verbs see pages 150-1.

- The contractions (in brackets) are used in speech and informal writing.

B Uses

- We use the present perfect for a situation that started in the past and continues to the present.

  *I'**ve worked** in marketing all my life.*
  *I'**ve known** Kumiko since we were at university together.*

- We use the present perfect to talk about a series of actions up to the present.

  *I'**ve visited** Spain several times.*
  *We **have made** many improvements to this software in the new version.*

- We use the present perfect for a past event that has a present result.

  *I'**ve lost** their invoice – I can't find it anywhere.*
  *Your taxi **has arrived**. See you again soon – have a safe journey!*

- In general, the present perfect connects the past with the present. The first two cases are 'life up to now' and the third is 'present result of a past action'.

- Notice that with the present perfect the time period is not finished or not definite.

  *I'**ve worked** in marketing all my life.*   (not finished – I continue to work in marketing)
  *I'**ve visited** Spain many times.*   (not definite – no time given)
  *I'**ve lost** their invoice.*   (not definite – no time given)

  Compare with the past simple (unit 4) where the time is finished and definite.

"This is goodbye, gentlemen. I have met another board of directors, and we have fallen in love."

C *Been* and *gone*

- Notice the difference between *has been to* and *has gone to*.

  *She'**s been to** Paris* means she went there and has now returned.
  *She'**s gone to** Paris* means she went there but has not yet returned. She is still there.

Exercises

6.1 Complete this verb table of irregular verbs. The last letter has been given to help you. Check on pages 150-1.

	Infinitive	Past simple	Past participle		Infinitive	Past simple	Past participle
1	be	was	_____been_	9	have	had	_____d
2	begin	began	_____n	10	know	knew	_____n
3	buy	bought	_____t	11	make	made	_____e
4	come	came	_____e	12	meet	met	_____t
5	do	did	_____e	13	see	saw	_____n
6	get	got	_____t	14	think	thought	_____t
7	give	gave	_____n	15	take	took	_____n
8	go	went	_____e	16	write	wrote	_____n

6.2 Complete this extract from an Annual Report using these verbs in the present perfect: *be, begin, buy, ~~have~~, make.*

Annual Report

I am pleased to report that we (1) _____have had_____ an excellent year. Our financial services division (2) _____ a profit of over eight million dollars, and for the first time we (3) _____ activities in the area of life insurance. Our expansion plans in Central Europe are also going well: senior managers (4) _____ there many times over the year to look at the possibilities of setting up subsidiaries, and in Slovakia we (5) _____ a controlling share in an existing local company.

6.3 Complete this email by putting the verbs into the present perfect. There are affirmative, negative and question forms.

Subject | construction of new line for Bucharest metro

Jim – (1) _____*have you heard*_____ (you/hear) about the plans to extend the Bucharest metro? The European Union (2) _____ (announce) that they will provide funding for another line. All construction companies are invited to make a bid. Several points occur to me:

1. Our big competitors like Alstom and Bechtel (3) _____ (not/make) any public statements yet, but I'm sure they will be interested.

2. What about us? Should we put in our own bid? I (4) _____ (prepare) a short report with my own ideas. It's attached to this email. Let me know what you think.

3. It would be good to talk to Dimitrie about this, but he (5) _____ (not/reply) to my last few emails. (6) _____ (you/see) him recently?

Anyway, my secretary will schedule a meeting on this issue at the end of March. Please discuss the matter with your team members before then.

"And now, for all of you out there who are in love, or if you've ever been in love, or if you think you'll be in love someday, or even if you only think you might like to be in love someday, this song is for you."

A   Ever/never

● We use *ever* and *never* to talk about life experience. *Ever* is used in questions.

*Have you **ever** worked abroad?*   (in your life up to now)
*I've **never** been to the United States.*   (in my life up to now)

● A question with *ever* in the present perfect is often followed by an answer in the past simple. The past simple refers to a completed time period.

*A: **Have** you **ever worked** abroad?*
*B: Yes, I have. I **worked** for a bank in London. That **was** about ten years ago.*

B   Already/yet

● We use *already* in affirmative sentences to mean 'earlier than expected'. Note the position.

*She's **already** spoken to me.* (NOT ~~She's spoken already to me.~~)

● We use *yet* in questions and negatives. It means 'something hasn't happened, but I expect it to happen'. Note the positions.

*Have you spoken to her **yet**?* (NOT ~~Have you spoken yet to her?~~)
*She hasn't spoken to me **yet**.* (NOT ~~She hasn't spoken yet to me.~~)

C   Just

● We use *just* to mean 'a short time ago'.

*I'm sorry, he's **just** left.*

D   For/since

*Oracle **has dominated** the database business **for more than two decades.***

World Trade Magazine website

● We use *for* to talk about the length of a time period.

*I've worked here **for** six months.*

● We use *since* to talk about when the time period started.

*I've worked here **since** 2004.*

● *For* can also be used with the past simple for a completed time period.

*I **worked** in London **for a few years** in the 1990s.*

E   Unfinished periods of time

*The dollar **has fallen** significantly **over the past three years** against the euro. **This week**, a euro **has been worth** about $1.30.*

msnbc website

● We use the present perfect with time adverbs that refer to a period that has not finished: *today, this month, this year, so far, up to now, over the last few years*, etc.

*I've **had** three long meetings **today**.*   (it is mid-afternoon – the day is not finished)
*Sales **this year have increased** by 5%.*   (it is October – the year is not finished)
*I've **written** half the report **so far/up to now**.* (there is still more time left for writing)

Exercises

7.1   Complete each sentence with one of these time adverbs: ~~already~~, *ever, for, just, never, since, so far, yet.*

1   The project is going very well – we've __*already*__ finished phase one.

2   I haven't finished the July sales report _____

3   Sorry, I've been really busy – I've been in a meeting _____ nine o'clock.

4   I'm a bit nervous – I've _____ spoken to so many people before.

5   We've known each other _____ more than twenty years.

6   We've had 120 registrations for the conference _____ , and the maximum is 150.

7   Have you _____ eaten sushi?

8   I've _____ heard about your promotion! Congratulations!

7.2   Put the verbs into the present perfect or past simple.

1   A: __*Have you ever been*__ (you/ever/be) to Latin America?

    B: Just once. I _____ (go) on a walking holiday in Patagonia.

2   A: _____ (you/ever/use) the London Underground?

    B: Yes, I have. I remember the voice that _____ (say) 'Mind The Gap'.

3   A: _____ (you/ever/give) a presentation to a large audience?

    B: Yes, I have. It _____ (not/be) too bad after I _____ (start).

7.3   Complete the sentences with *for* or *since*.

1   I've been at KPMG _____ nearly a year, _____ January in fact.

2   I haven't heard from her _____ the beginning of the month. So _____ the last
    few weeks I haven't been able to do anything.

3   I've known Rafik _____ a long time, _____ we were at university together.

7.4   Susan is speaking to her friend on the phone at lunchtime. Complete what she says using these words:
already, ever, for, just, never, since, up to now, ~~yet~~.

What a terrible day! I haven't replied to all my emails (1) ___*yet*___
and I've been here (2) _____ eight o'clock. And I have to write
a report this afternoon. My boss has (3) _____ reminded me about
it three times this week. Honestly, I've been in this job (4) _____
three years and I've (5) _____ had so much work to do.
(6) _____ I haven't complained, but if things continue like this, I'm
going to say something. Oh sorry, I have to go now. I've (7) _____
seen my boss come in and I don't want him to hear me chatting on the
phone. Maybe we could go out for a drink one evening. Have you
(8) _____ been to that Salsa Bar near the cathedral? They say it's
very good. Anyway, speak to you soon. Bye.

A Past simple or present perfect?

● Here is a summary of units 4 and 6:

Past simple	Present perfect
- time period finished I **lived** in Berlin when I was young.	- time period not finished I've **lived** in Berlin all my life.
- time period definite I **visited** Berlin last week. 'Definite' time period means we know when the action happened (*last week*)	- time period not definite I've **visited** Berlin several times. 'Not definite' means the exact time of the action is not given and not important (*several times*)
- telling a story I **lost** my passport. It was a big problem. In the end, we **won** the contract. These sentences use *lost* and *won* because the attention of the speaker is in the past. The speaker is telling a story about past events.	- present result I've **lost** my passport. Have you seen it? We've **won** the contract! Congratulations! These sentences use *have lost* and *have won* because the attention of the speaker is in the present: looking for the passport now, celebrating the good news about the contract now.

B Time adverbs

● Time adverbs help us to choose between past simple and present perfect.

Last year profits **increased** by 6%.   **This year** profits **have increased** by 2%.
('last year' is finished)   ('this year' is not finished)

In 1998 I **changed** my job.   I've **changed** my job. I'm working for Nokia now.
('in 1998' is definite)   (no definite time is given for the job change)

● Review units 4 and 7 for time adverbs.

C Present simple or present perfect?

● If we are talking about a general situation with no particular time reference in our mind, we use the present simple.

I **live** in Berlin.
We **win** many contracts.

● If we connect the past to the present, we use the present perfect. We mention an unfinished time period or talk about a present result.

I've **lived** in Berlin for many years.
We've just **won** the contract for the Bucharest metro.

Exercises

8.1 Match each sentence with situation a) or b).

1 Inflation rose by 2%. ☐   a) Last year it was 3%. This year it is 5%.
2 Inflation has risen by 2%. ☐   b) Two years ago it was 3%. Last year it was 5%.

3 Has Bill called this morning? ☐   a) Bill said he would call. It's eleven am.
4 Did Bill call this morning? ☐   b) Bill said he would call. It's two pm.

5 Sue had an accident. ☐   a) Quick – call an ambulance!
6 Sue has had an accident. ☐   b) So we came back from our vacation early.

9 **8.2** Complete this article by putting three verbs into the past simple and three into the present perfect.

Nike: the brand that keeps growing

An accountant and a sports coach (1) ___started___ (start) a small shoe company called Blue Ribbon in 1964. In 1971 it (2) _____ (change) its name to Nike, and since then it (3) _____ (become) one of the world's most successful brands. Originally Nike (4) _____ (be) only associated with basketball, but recently it (5) _____ (expand) into new markets like football. Now Nike (6) _____ (start) buying other fashion brands that are not even connected with sport.

8.3 <u>Underline</u> the correct words.

1 Their share price *goes up/went up/has gone up* by 4% yesterday.
2 Their share price *goes up/went up/has gone up* by 4% today.
3 Their share price *goes up/went up/has gone up* every month.
4 *I live/I lived/I've lived* in Barcelona since the end of last year.
5 *I live/I lived/I've lived* in Barcelona now – it's a great city.
6 *I live/I lived/I've lived* in Barcelona when I was a student.
7 When I cross the road in London *I forget/I forgot/I've forgotten* to look the right way.
8 Oh no! *I forget/I forgot/I've forgotten* her name! Can you remember it?
9 I must call Laura. *I forget/I forgot/I've forgotten* to thank her for the meal last night.

10 **8.4** Simon is talking to a colleague about a business trip. Complete what he says by putting four verbs into the past simple and four into the present perfect.

I (1) ___have just come___ (just/come) back from Vietnam. It (2) _____ (be) fascinating. Over recent years the Japanese (3) _____ (invest) a lot of money in the country – we (4) _____ (see) their factories all along the coast. But I'm really tired now – my flight (5) _____ (arrive) yesterday and I (6) _____ (not/recover) from the trip yet. And I got a shock this morning when I (7) _____ (turn) on my computer – I (8) _____ (never/see) so many emails in my inbox!

Present perfect continuous

A Form

- We form the present perfect continuous with *has/have + been* + the *-ing* form of the verb.

Affirmative	Negative	Question
I have ('ve) been working	*I have not (haven't) been working*	*Have I been working?*
You have ('ve) been working	*You have not (haven't) been working*	*Have you been working?*
He/she/it has ('s) been working	*He/she/it has not (hasn't) been working*	*Has he/she/it been working?*
We have ('ve) been working	*We have not (haven't) been working*	*Have we been working?*
They have ('ve) been working	*They have not (haven't) been working*	*Have they been working?*

- The contractions (in brackets) are used in speech and informal writing.

B Uses

- We use the present perfect continuous for an action or situation in progress from a time in the past up to now.

  *Sales **have been falling** slowly over the last few years.*
  *I've **been thinking** about your suggestion all week.*

- Notice from the examples above that we often use a time adverb to state the duration of the situation in progress: *over the last few years, all week, for ten years, for ages, since nine o'clock,* etc.

- The action may continue into the future or not; we only know from the context.

  *Here you are at last! I've **been waiting** for ages!* (the waiting is finished)
  *I've **been waiting** for ages! I'll stay just five minutes more.* (I will continue waiting)

C Present perfect or present perfect continuous?

- When we talk about 'life up to now' we can normally use the present perfect or present perfect continuous with little change in meaning.

  *I've **worked**/I've **been working** here for two years.* (no real difference)
  *I've **lived**/I've **been living** in Prague since last summer.* (no real difference)

- When we talk about a 'present result', we use the present perfect.

  *I've **done** the accounts. They're on the desk.* (the finished accounts are in my mind)

  But when our attention is on the action itself, not the result, we use the present perfect continuous.

  *I need a break. I've **been doing** the accounts all morning.* (the 'doing' is in my mind)

- If we say 'how many' we normally use the present perfect, not the continuous form.

  *I've **written three reports** this week.* (NOT ~~I've been writing~~)
  *It's **taken two hours** to get here.* (NOT ~~It's been taking~~)

- Remember from unit 3 that state verbs like *know, understand, hear, like* do not normally have a continuous form. (NOT ~~I've been knowing Kate for ten years.~~)

Exercises

9.1 Put the verbs into the correct form of the present perfect continuous.

1 How long _have you been learning_ (you/learn) English?

2 The price of oil _____ (go up) steadily since the nineties.

3 Use another scanner – that one _____ (not/work) for ages.

4 I _____ (try) to call Keiko all morning, but there's no reply.

5 _____ (you/service) this machine regularly?

9.2 In each sentence put one verb into the present perfect and the other into the present perfect continuous.

1 I _have been looking_ (look) through the contract all morning and I _____have noticed_____ (notice) one or two points that need clarification.

2 We _____ (make) cars on this site for over six years. This financial year we _____ (invest) over $4 million in a new production line.

3 She _____ (lose) her cell phone – she _____ (look) for it since lunchtime.

4 We _____ (email) each other all week and I think that we _____ (make) real progress with the whole planning process.

9.3 Put a tick (✓) by four sentences that are possible. Put a cross (✗) by two that are not.

1 I've studied French at evening class for three years. ✓

2 I've been studying French at evening class for three years.

3 We've spent 20,000 euros on this promotion.

4 We've been spending 20,000 euros on this promotion.

5 The contract is complicated, but I think I've understood it now.

6 The contract is complicated, but I think I've been understanding it now.

9.4 Look at this extract from a meeting. There are eight verb forms in *italics*. Cross out the two that are not possible.

OK, shall we start? *I've asked you/I've been asking you* to come to this meeting to discuss possible candidates for promotion. Top of my list is Hanna. *She's led/She's been leading* her team very effectively all year, and over recent months *she's completed/she's been completing* two difficult negotiations. I know that other team leaders *have worked/have been working* hard as well, but I feel that Hanna deserves our special attention. Karen, would you like to make a few comments to open the discussion?

 **Past perfect**

A Form

● We form the past perfect with the auxiliary *had* + the past participle of the verb.

Affirmative	Negative	Question
I had ('d) worked	*I had not (hadn't) worked*	*Had I worked?*
You had ('d) worked	*You had not (hadn't) worked*	*Had you worked?*
He/she/it had ('d) worked	*He/she/it had not (hadn't) worked*	*Had he/she/it worked?*
We had ('d) worked	*We had not (hadn't) worked*	*Had we worked?*
They had ('d) worked	*They had not (hadn't) worked*	*Had they worked?*

● We use contractions (in brackets) in speech and informal writing.

B Uses

● Compare these two situations:

1 We arrived at their offices at 9.00. The meeting started at 9.02.

We say: *When we **arrived** at their offices, the meeting **started**.* (both verbs in past simple)

2 We arrived at their offices at 9.00. The meeting started at 8.55.

We say: *When we **arrived** at their offices, the meeting **had started**.* (second verb in past perfect)

● So the past perfect is used to emphasize that one past event happens before another. We use the past perfect for the earlier event.

● The past perfect is often used after verbs of thinking such as: *think, know, be sure, realize, remember, understand,* etc.

*I **thought** I'**d seen** him somewhere before, but I was wrong.*
*He **knew** he'**d made** a mistake.*
*When I got to the airport, I **remembered** I **hadn't closed** the kitchen window.*

C Time adverbs

● With the past perfect we often use *already, never* and *by.*

*When I arrived at the conference centre, her presentation **had already started**.*
*You won't believe it – I forgot my passport! I'**d never done** that before.*
***By** the end of the day I **had interviewed** six candidates for the job.*

● It is not necessary to use the past perfect if we use *before* or *after* to make the time sequence clear.

*The meeting (**had**) **started before** we arrived.* (had is optional here)
*We arrived **after** the meeting (**had**) **started**.* (had is optional here)

Exercises

10.1 <u>Underline</u> the two past perfect forms in the text. Then tick (✓) the correct time sequence.

> I was really tired because I'd been at the restaurant until one o'clock. I woke up at half past ten the next morning and realized that I hadn't heard the alarm clock go off.

1   being tired → the restaurant → waking up → not hearing alarm clock
2   the restaurant → being tired → waking up → not hearing alarm clock
3   the restaurant → being tired → not hearing alarm clock → waking up

10.2 One verb in each sentence should be in the past perfect. Write the correction.

1   When I *got* to the meeting, I *realized* that I *left* all my papers behind. *had left*
2   I *went* to Manchester and *saw* that they *converted* all the old warehouses into apartments.
3   I *was* sure I *didn't receive* the invoice, but I *checked* one more time.
4   I really *enjoyed* my holiday in Peru – I *visited* Latin America several times before, but only for short business trips. We *saw* the Nazca Lines and Machu Picchu.
5   I *was* lucky – I *arrived* at the hall late, but her presentation *didn't start*.

10.3 Complete the first line in two ways, either using *so* + past simple or *because* + past perfect.

1   I had no success when I tried to contact Katarina …
   a. (I/speak/to her colleague instead) _so I spoke to her colleague instead._
   b. (she/move/to another company) _because she had moved to another company._
2   My boss was in a very good mood today …
   a. (he/negotiate/a better price for some components) _____
   b. (I/ask/him for a pay rise) _____
3   The parts arrived ten days late …
   a. (we/decide/to look for another supplier) _____
   b. (there/be/a strike at the factory) _____

10.4 Antonio is talking about his career. Put three verbs into the past simple and three verbs into the past perfect.

> I (1) _____started_____ (start) working as a freelance consultant in 2004, but before that I (2) _____ (already/work) as a software engineer in the telecommunications industry for many years. One day I (3) _____ (realize) that I (4) _____ (gain) enough experience to start up in business on my own, so I (5) _____ (leave) the telecoms company. They were very sad because I (6) _____ (be) one of their best employees.

Units 1–10 of this book explain past and present verb forms. The text and diagrams below summarise the information in a different way.

A Simple forms

The past simple describes one completed action in the past, or a completed situation that lasted for a period of time. The present simple describes things that are always or usually true, so it is shown by the whole horizontal line.

Past simple   Past simple   NOW

P r e s e n t   s i m p l e

I worked at Telecom for three years.   *I spoke to Mary yesterday.*   *I live in Tokyo.*

B Continuous forms

The past continuous and present continuous both have the meaning of an action in progress. Remember that state verbs (*know, like, want*) are not normally used in a continuous form (unit 3).

NOW

Past continuous   Present continuous

While we were testing the new drug we discovered …   *We're developing two new products at the moment.*

C Perfect forms

The past perfect and present perfect both have the meaning of looking back. The past perfect looks back from the past and the present perfect looks back from the present.

NOW

Past perfect   Present perfect

The meeting had already started when I arrived.   *I've been in this job for three years.*

Exercises

13 **11.1** Complete the dialogue by putting two verbs in the past simple (*I did*) and two in the present perfect (*I have done*).

MARCUS: I (1) _____ (have) a meeting with Andy Wilkinson yesterday. He mentioned your name. I (2) _____ (never/do) business with him before.

FRANK: Oh, I (3) _____ (know) Andy all my life. Actually we (4) _____ (go) to university together. He's a good guy – you can trust him.

14 **11.2** Complete the dialogue by putting two verbs in the present simple (*I do*), two in the present continuous (*I am doing*), and two in the present perfect (*I have done*).

ALICIA: Hi, Joelle. How are things at the Paris office? And when are you going to come to Frankfurt? Every year you (1) _____*say*_____ (say) you will visit us, but you never do!

JOELLE: The thing is, we're really busy at the moment. Right now we (2) _____ (prepare) all the promotional materials for the new range of summer clothes.

ALICIA: Yes, I (3) _____ (see) the designs – they look really great. I'm sure they will sell really well in Germany.

JOELLE: Thanks for the feedback. We (4) _____ (work) quite hard over the last few months. As well as preparing the summer range, this year we (5) _____ (try) to develop some new distribution channels. We (6) _____ (want) to cut out the wholesalers and sell directly to large stores.

ALICIA: Yes, I heard something about that.

15 **11.3** Complete the dialogue by putting two verbs in the present perfect (*I have done*), two in the past perfect (*I had done*), and two in the past continuous (*I was doing*).

ROBERTO: Excuse me, Mr. Andersen, can I come in? I tried to speak to you earlier, but you (1) __*had already gone*__ (already/go) to lunch.

MR ANDERSEN: Yes, of course, please come in. I (2) _____ (just/look) at these sales figures for the third quarter. Would you like a coffee?

ROBERTO: No thanks, I (3) _____ (just/have) one.

MR ANDERSEN: So, what did you come to see me about?

ROBERTO: Well, I'm probably getting worried for no reason – but while I (4) _____ (speak) to Fernando he mentioned that he (5) _____ (hear) some rumours that the whole Latin American division is going to be reorganized. Is that true?

MR ANDERSEN: No, no, there (6) _____ (be) a misunderstanding. We are going to make some changes at senior management level, but there will be no impact on day-to-day operations. I'll clarify the situation at the meeting tomorrow.

12 Future 1: *will*

A Form

● We use *will* + the infinitive (without *to*).

Affirmative	I/you/he/she/it/we/they **will work**
Negative	I/you/he/she/it/we/they **won't work**
Question	**Will** I/you/he/she/it/we/they **work?**

"Let me get this, but keep in mind that you'll pay for it in other, more subtle ways later on."

● *Will* is usually shortened in speech and informal writing to *'ll*.

B Facts and predictions

● We can use *will* on its own for something certain in the future, a fact.

*The store **will be** closed on Sunday.*
*I'll **be** 40 next year.*

● But usually the future is not certain, and instead we have to make a prediction based on our opinions and beliefs. To do this we add a verb at the beginning like: *believe, be sure, expect, hope, know, suppose, think*.

*I **think** inflation **will go up** next year.*
*I **hope** they'll **agree** to the deal.*

We can also use adverbs like *probably* and *definitely*. Note the positions.

*She'll **probably be** at the meeting.*   (will + probably)
*She **probably won't be** at the meeting.*   (probably + won't)

C Instant decisions, promises, offers, requests

● We also use *will* when we decide to do something more or less at the moment of speaking.

instant decision	*I'll **wait** for you outside.*
promises	*I'll **do** the best I can.*
offers of help	*I'll **carry** your suitcase to the car.*
requests	***Will** you **get** me an espresso, please?*

● In real life these separate uses are often combined.

*OK, I'll **email** the information to you.* (an instant decision and a promise)

D Talking about the future

● There are several ways to talk about the future in English:

will	*Bye! I'll **see** you tomorrow.*	unit 12 and 14
going to	*I'm **going to meet** her next week.*	unit 13 and 14
present continuous	*I'm **meeting** her at nine next Friday.*	unit 13 and 14
present simple	*My flight **arrives** at half past ten.*	unit 14
modal verbs	*I **might meet** her next week.*	unit 25

Exercises

12.1 Add one of these words to each sentence, in the correct place: *expect, sure, probably, probably*.

1 I'm we'll have to increase our prices.

2 I we'll have to increase our prices.

3 We'll have to increase our prices.

4 We won't have to increase our prices.

12.2 Replace the <u>underlined</u> words with a form of *will*. Use contractions where possible.

1 I <u>promise to</u> speak to my boss about it. _____*I'll speak to my boss about it.*_____

2 I <u>promise not to</u> discuss this with anyone. _____

3 I <u>offer to</u> meet you at the station. _____

4 It's no good – they <u>refuse to</u> negotiate. _____

5 Mrs Okada is on another line – <u>I request that</u> you hold. _____

6 We need some fresh air. I<u>'ve just decided to</u> open a window. _____

7 If you <u>aren't willing to</u> tell him the truth, I <u>am</u>. _____

8 I<u>'m not</u> here next week. I<u>'m</u> in Stockholm. _____

12.3 Match comments 1–4 with instant responses a)–d).

1 Can I get you anything? ☐   a) Don't worry, I'll deal with it.

2 It's a difficult situation. ☐   b) Yes, I think I'll stop now.

3 I'm afraid the line is busy. ☐   c) I'll have a gin and tonic, please.

4 You've been working all day. ☐   d) OK, I'll call back later.

16

12.4 In this article, add the word *will* in eight places and the word *won't* in one place.

The future of work

What your office look like in twenty years' time? I expect there be just a small number of people, sitting on comfortable chairs, talking together and using hand-held computers. I think more people probably work as freelancers, and those still inside the company on permanent contracts have more flexible job descriptions. Both groups do more work from home, and via the Internet. In general, companies be smaller and more specialized. A consequence of all these trends is that the office become a place for 'face time' only – those occasions when meetings of real people are absolutely essential. But some things probably change. These days people want more from their work: they expect their jobs to be more interesting, creative and satisfying. And I think that this continue.

13 Future 2: *going to* and present continuous

"I'm afraid I'm going to be late home for dinner again, Mavis ... about three days"

A Going to

Affirmative	*I'm/you're/he's/she's/it's/we're/they're **going to work**.*
Negative	*I'm/you're/he's/she's/it's/we're/they're **not going to work**.*
Question	***Am** I/**are** you/**is** he/**is** she/**is** it/**are** we/**are** they **going to work**?*

● We use *be + going to + infinitive* to talk about plans and decisions that we have already made. The time can be near future or distant future.

I'm going to have a meeting with my bank manager tomorrow.
We're going to move all our production to Slovakia next year.

● We also use *going to* for predictions, especially when there is strong evidence in the present situation.

It's going to be difficult to increase market share. (there is a lot of competition)
It looks like inflation is going to fall next year. (this newspaper article says so)

B Present continuous

● The present continuous (*I am working/he is working*) is described in unit 2 with a present time reference. It also has a future time reference: to talk about fixed arrangements. There is nearly always a time phrase.

I'm catching the Eurostar to Brussels at 8.30 tomorrow morning.
Next year Miki is coming from the Tokyo office to join our team.

● The fixed arrangements are often social arrangements and appointments.

I'm playing tennis at 11.00, then after that I'm meeting Jim and Sue for lunch.

● Remember from unit 3 that state verbs (*think, know, want*) are not normally used in a continuous form.

C Going to or present continuous?

● There are many situations where we can use either *going to* or the present continuous. *Going to* is for plans, the present continuous is for arrangements – plans and arrangements are very similar.

I'm going to meet/I'm meeting her tomorrow.

● However there can be a small difference. *Going to* is more common where the details are not yet finalized – it's just a plan. The present continuous is more common where the details are fixed, with a time and a place – it's 'in our diary'.

I'm going to give a presentation at the conference. (exact details are still unknown)
I'm giving my presentation at 10.30 in room G12. (all the details are fixed)

Exercises

13.1 Decide how *going to* is used in each sentence. Write *plan* or *prediction* at the end.

1 It's going to be a difficult meeting.   *prediction*

2 I'm going to visit some clients in Helsinki next week.   _____

3 The new model looks fantastic. It's going to be a huge success.   _____

4 You want delivery by Friday? That's going to be difficult.   _____

5 After lunch we're going to look round the factory.   _____

13.2 Replace the underlined words with a form of *going to*.

1 I've decided to look for another job.   *I'm going to look for another job.*

2 We plan to patent this invention. _____

3 What do you intend to do? _____

4 They have decided not to have a stand at the Expo. _____

5 GSK intends to launch a new heart drug. _____

13.3 Read the evidence in the first sentence. Then use the words in brackets to make a prediction with *going to*.

1 People are living longer and having fewer children.

(the workforce/get older)   *The workforce is going to get older.*

2 Prices in the shops are rising.

(the trade unions/ask for higher wages) _____

3 We have to finish the project this month, but there's too much work to do.

(we/not have enough time) _____

4 That machine is making a strange noise again.

(I think it/break down) _____

13.4 Complete the dialogue by putting the verbs into the correct form of the present continuous. (See unit 2 for present continuous forms.)

SIMONE: Erica Morrison from Head Office (1) _____ *is coming* _____ (come) tomorrow to talk about marketing ideas for next year.

REMY: Good. What time (2) _____ (she/arrive)?

SIMONE: She (3) _____ (get) here at ten, then we (4) _____ (have) a meeting with the senior management team until about twelve.

REMY: (5) _____ (you/take) her out for lunch?

SIMONE: Yes. We (6) _____ (not/go) anywhere expensive – just a little Italian restaurant round the corner. Would you like to join us?

14 Future 3: review, present simple, future probability

A Review: *will*, *going to* and present continuous

● Here is a summary of units 12 and 13. But remember that in real life these differences are not so clear and different forms may be possible.

Will	*Going to*	**Present continuous**
Instant decision/ promise/offer: made at the moment of speaking	Plan made previously, before the moment of speaking	Fixed arrangement 'in our diary' with a time and a place
Prediction based on our opinions and beliefs	Prediction based on strong evidence in the present situation	

B Time adverbs

● With all forms of the future we use time adverbs like: *this evening, tonight, tomorrow, tomorrow morning, the day after tomorrow, at the weekend, next week, not this weekend but the next, soon, in a few days' time, a year from now.*

C Present simple

● The present simple can have a future time reference. We use it to talk about events based on a timetable, programme, schedule or calendar. In these cases we can also use the present continuous.

*Anton's plane **leaves/is leaving** at 12.00.*
*Our company **has/is having** its 50th anniversary next year.*

● We use the present simple to refer to the future after these words: *after, as soon as, before, if, in case, unless, until, when.*

As soon as *I **hear** anything, I'll let you know.*
*Our production manager will show you the new factory **before** you **leave**.*
*Please wait here **until** Mrs Hall **comes** back.*
When *I **arrive**, I'll call you.*

D Future probability

● We can use these phrases to express degrees of certainty about the future.

100% *be certain to*   90% *be expected to*   80% *be likely to*   20% *be unlikely to*

OPEC **is expected to** *maintain current levels of oil production.*
*The Federal Reserve **is likely to** lower interest rates.*

● We can use the modal verbs *may, might* and *could* to express a future probability of about 50%. (See unit 25.)

*When we raise our prices next month, we **may/might/could** see a fall in sales.*
*I **may not/might not** meet my sales targets this quarter.*

Exercises

14.1 Put the verbs into the future. Choose *will* or *going to*. Use contractions.

OLGA: I'm out of the office this afternoon. (1) _____ (I/visit) a customer.

EMIL: OK, (2) _____ (I/answer) your phone if it rings. Do you want to borrow my umbrella? The weather forecast says (3) _____ (it/rain).

OLGA: Oh, thanks a lot. (4) _____ (I/give) it back to you tomorrow.

14.2 Complete this telephone dialogue. Put three verbs into the *will* future and three into the present continuous. Use contractions.

NINA: Hi Ernesto. Nice to hear from you. How are things in Mexico City?

ERNESTO: Oh, everything's fine here, thanks. Look, (1) _____*I'll be*_____ (I/be) in LA for a few days next week – (2) _____*I'm arriving*_____ (I/arrive) at the airport on Tuesday morning, and I thought it would be useful if we could have a meeting at some point.

NINA: Yes, good idea. Let me see. The day you arrive is not very good for me – (3) _____ (I/have) lunch with a trade delegation from South Korea and I think (4) _____ (we/probably/continue) the discussions during the afternoon. How about Wednesday morning?

ERNESTO: OK. On Wednesday (5) _____ (I/see) someone at twelve, but before that I'm free. So shall we say 9.00?

NINA: That's fine. (6) _____ (I/call) you Tuesday evening to confirm it.

14.3 In each sentence put one verb into the *will* future and one into the present simple.

1 I expect our share price _____*will rise*_____ (rise) when we _____*announce*_____ (announce) the sales figures.

2 As soon as the goods _____ (arrive), I _____ (call) you.

3 Don't worry, I _____ (turn off) the lights before I _____ (leave).

4 When we _____ (upgrade) the website, you _____ (be able to) order online.

5 After we _____ (pay) all our taxes, we _____ (have) very little money left for reinvesting in the business.

"I'LL INTRODUCE YOU TO THESE PEOPLE AS SOON AS SOMEBODY TELLS ME WHO THEY ARE."

14.4 Complete the sentences with the correct form of *be certain to, be likely to,* or *be unlikely to.*

1 Jane _____ do well. She's often late and is sometimes rude to other staff.

2 Jane _____ do well. She's confident, intelligent and hard-working.

3 Jane _____ do well, although she's still young and has a lot to learn.

A Yes/no questions

● The table below is a summary. (Full forms are given in earlier units.)

present simple	*Do you live in Prague?*	*Does she live in Prague?*
present continuous	*Are you coming with us?*	*Is he coming with us?*
past simple	*Did you go to the meeting?*	*Did she go to the meeting?*
past continuous	*Were you waiting long?*	*Was he waiting long?*
present perfect	*Have you ever eaten sushi?*	*Has he ever eaten sushi?*
present perfect continuous	*Have you been working?*	*Has she been working?*
past perfect	*Had you left when I called?*	*Had she left when I called?*
modals: *can/could/will*	*Can you speak German?*	*Can he speak German?*

● Notice that *yes/no* questions are formed with an auxiliary verb + subject + main verb. The auxiliary can be *do, be, have* or a modal verb like *can, will*, etc.

● Notice that to make a question we take the affirmative form and then invert the subject and the auxiliary.

*He **is** working*	→	***Is** he working?*
*She **has** worked*	→	***Has** she worked?*
*He **was** working*	→	***Was** he working?*
*She **has been** working*	→	***Has** she **been** working?*
*He **had** worked*	→	***Had** he worked?*
*She **can** work*	→	***Can** she work?*

"Oh, by the way, do you have any money? Will you send me any money? Do you know anyone who has any money? Will they send me any money?"

● The present simple and past simple do not have an auxiliary in the affirmative form. So to keep the pattern we use *do* and *did*.

| *She works* | → | ***Does** she work?* | (NOT ~~Works she?~~) |
| *He worked* | → | ***Did** he work?* | (NOT ~~Worked he?~~) |

B Short answers

● To make a short answer we repeat the auxiliary verb, not the main verb.

A: *Do you speak French?*	B: *Yes, I do./No, I don't.*	(NOT ~~Yes, I speak.~~)
A: *Are you staying at the Ritz?*	B: *Yes, I am./No, I'm not.*	(NOT ~~Yes, I staying.~~)
A: *Did you see Michel?*	B: *Yes, I did./No, I didn't.*	(NOT ~~Yes, I saw.~~)
A: *Were you enjoying yourself?*	B: *Yes, I was./No, I wasn't.*	
A: *Have you read this report?*	B: *Yes, I have./No, I haven't.*	
A: *Have you been waiting long?*	B: *Yes, I have./No, I haven't.*	
A: *Had you met him before?*	B: *Yes, I had./No, I hadn't.*	
A: *Can you be here at 7.00?*	B: *Yes, I can./No, I can't.*	
A: *Will you be late?*	B: *Yes, I will./No, I won't.*	

Exercises

15.1 Change each affirmative sentence into a question.

1 Bill thinks it's a good idea.   *Does Bill think it's a good idea?*
2 Sonia is arriving on Monday.   _____
3 He made a copy of the Excel file.   _____
4 They've offered her the job.   _____
5 She'll be at the meeting tomorrow.   _____

15.2 Read the replies, then complete the questions about the operating system Linux.

1 A: *Were you reading about IBM?*   B: IBM? No, I was reading about Linux.
2 A: _____   B: Linux? No, most servers use Windows.
3 A: _____   B: Falling? No, the popularity of Linux is growing.
4 A: _____   B: The eighties? No, Linux started in 1991.
5 A: _____   B: On our computers? No, we haven't installed it.
6 A: _____   B: A lot of money? No, the inventor hasn't been making a lot. The software is free!

15.3 Write a short reply for each question, beginning as shown.

1 Did you speak to Kate? Yes, _____ *I did.* _____
2 Have you been to Brazil? No, _____
3 Do you play golf? Yes, _____
4 Does Bill play golf? No, _____
5 Did you have a good trip? Yes, _____
6 Can you speak German? No, _____
7 Are you coming with us? Yes, _____
8 Is Maria coming with us? No, _____

15.4 Complete the dialogue with these words: *are, do, does, did, has, have, is*.

MIKE: (1) _____ you go to the training day they told us about at the last meeting?

SUE: (2) _____ you talking about the computer training?

MIKE: No, not the computer training, I meant the sales training.

SUE: Oh yes, I went to that. It was quite good. (3) _____ you ever been on that course?

MIKE: No, I haven't.

SUE: Well I found it very useful. It helps you to think about the type of questions we ask our clients during a sales conversation.

MIKE: When you go on these courses (4) _____ the company pay or (5) _____ you pay yourself? I know that good training isn't cheap.

SUE: Oh, the company pays – they can afford it. It doesn't cost us anything.

MIKE: And (6) _____ it helped you in your day-to-day work? Be honest now.

SUE: Yes, I think it has.

MIKE: OK. I'm interested. (7) _____ the course running again in the near future?

So you want to start a business. Do you have what it takes to succeed? (Part 2)

1 Are you a hard worker?

A Yes, I do whatever it takes to get the job done.

B No, life is too short. My free time is as important as my work.

2 Are you enthusiastic and energetic?

A Yes, I'm a tireless worker who looks forward to new challenges and tasks.

B No, I run out of energy sooner than most of my friends do.

3 Do you like to sell?

A Yes, especially when I sell something I believe in – I feel as though I have done the customer a service.

B No. Actually, I believe a good product or service should sell itself.

Asian Women in Business website

A   Saying *yes*

● Short replies can stop a conversation. Adding information can help to develop the conversation and the relationship. In place of a one-word *yes*, we could say:

A: *Is this your first visit to Bucharest?*	B: *Yes, that's right. I like the city very much.*
A: *Is this your first visit to Bucharest?*	B: *Yes, it is. I've always wanted to come here.*
A: *Do you want some help?*	B: *Oh, thanks very much. I'd appreciate that.*
A: *Do you want some help?*	B: *Yes, please. That's very kind of you.*
A: *May I use your photocopier?*	B: *Of course. Go right ahead.*
A: *May I use your photocopier?*	B: *Please do. It's at the end of the corridor.*
A: *Can you deliver by the end of May?*	B: *Yes, of course. That's no problem.*
A: *Can you deliver by the end of May?*	B: *Sure. We'd be happy to do that.*

B   Saying *no*

● In conversation, a one-word reply *no* is impolite. In place of a one-word *no*, we could say:

A: *Is this your first visit to Bucharest?*	B: *No, it isn't. I was here last June.*
A: *Is this your first visit to Bucharest?*	B: *No, I come here quite often.*
A: *Do you want some help?*	B: *No, thanks. I'm fine.*
A: *Do you want some help?*	B: *No, but thanks for asking.*
A: *May I use your photocopier?*	B: *I'm sorry, but it's not working.*
A: *May I use your photocopier?*	B: *Actually, it's not a good time right now.*
A: *Can you deliver by the end of May?*	B: *To be honest, that would be very difficult.*
A: *Can you deliver by the end of May?*	B: *May? I'm not sure we can do that.*

● In British English we can say *I'm afraid …* in place of *I'm sorry but …*

C   Disagreeing politely

● There are several ways to disagree politely. Study these ways to disagree with the comment: *I think we should cancel the whole project.*

question	*Really? Do you think so?* *What about the cost?*
negative question	*Don't you think there's another solution?* *Won't that be quite expensive?*
yes, but …	*I know what you're saying, but …* *I understand your point of view, but …*
introductory phrase	*Actually/To be honest, I can see one or two problems with that.* *I'm sorry, but I don't think that's a good idea.* *I'm afraid that's just not possible.*

Exercises

16.1 Write one word in each gap. The first letter has been given to help you.

1 A: Are you the new IT person?   B: Yes, that's r___*ight*___ . I started work last week.

2 A: Can I take a copy of this document?   B: Of c_____ . Go right a_____

3 A: Can I speak to you about Joe?   B: A_____ , it's not a good time right now.

4 A: Can I give you a lift to the station?   B: Thanks. That's very k_____ of you.

5 A: Do you want a hand with your bags?   B: Yes, please, I'd a_____ that.

6 A: May I help?   B: No, but thanks for a_____

7 A: Can we have a two-year warranty?   B: I'm a_____ I can't do that.

8 A: Can you modify the dimensions?   B: To be h_____ , that would be difficult.

16.2 Match each question 1–4 with an affirmative (+) and a negative (-) reply.

1 Can you give us 60 days credit?   a) Sure. That's no problem.
   (+) _a_ (–) _f_   b) Yes, please, I'd love one.

2 Would you like a cup of coffee?   c) Of course. Go right ahead.
   (+) ____ (–) ____   d) Yes, that's right.

3 Is this your only office in China?   e) No, thanks. I'm fine.
   (+) ____ (–) ____   f) 60 days? I'm not sure I can do that.

4 May I use your computer?   g) No, it isn't. We have two others.
   (+) ____ (–) ____   h) Sorry, it's not a good time right now.

16.3 Complete this customer-supplier dialogue using the phrases in the box.

> *Actually   Yes, of course   Yes, that's right   I'm fine*
> *That's just not possible   I know what you're saying*

ESTELLE: Thanks for coming here today. Would you like a drink – a coffee perhaps?

PATRICK: No thanks, (1) _____

ESTELLE : OK, I'd like to go over some details with you before we make a firm order.

PATRICK : (2) _____

ESTELLE : First, can I just confirm that the price you're quoting is $495 per unit?

PATRICK : (3) _____

ESTELLE : That seems quite expensive. It's right at the top end of our budget.

PATRICK : (4) _____ , it's not expensive. Not when you consider the quality.

ESTELLE : Maybe, but with the increased size of our order we were looking for a better price.

PATRICK : (5) _____ , but we've already given you a good discount.

ESTELLE : What about the shipping costs? Couldn't you include them in the price?

PATRICK : Include the shipping costs? I'm sorry. (6) _____

A Question words: *wh-* and *how*

- *Yes/no* questions are explained in unit 15. We can also make questions with a question word: *what, which, why, when, where, who, whose, how, how many, how much, how often.*

- Compare *what* + noun and *which* + noun:

What + noun	*Which* + noun
- *what* is more common for things *What software do you use?*	- *which* is more common for people and organizations *Which speaker is giving the opening talk?* *Which company do you work for?*
- *what* is more common where there is a wide choice *What time are you arriving?*	- *which* is more common where there is a limited number of choices *Which airport are you arriving at: Heathrow, Gatwick or Stansted?*

- *Whose* is used to ask who someone or something belongs to.
  ***Whose computers** are working, and **whose** are not working?*

- We can use *how* with adjectives: *How far, How important, How long,* etc.

- We use *how many* for countable nouns (dollars, bottles, people) and *How much* for uncountable nouns (money, water, information). (See unit 39.)

B Questions starting with a *wh-* or *how* word

- To make a question with a question word, we use the question word followed by exactly the same structure as a *yes/no* question (unit 15).

  So: question word + auxiliary verb + subject + main verb.

present simple	***When do** you usually **leave** work?*
present continuous	***What are** you **doing** about the Alpha project?*
past simple	***How did** you **feel** when you heard the news?*
past continuous	***Where were** you **living** at the time?*
present perfect	***Why have** you **stopped** selling that product?*
present perfect continuous	***Which** advertising agency **have** you **been using**?*
past perfect	***Who had** they **told** before they announced it publicly?*
can/could/will	***What can** I **say**? **What will** you **do**?*

"Hey, this is brilliant! Where do you get my ideas?"

C Prepositions in questions

- In modern English we move the preposition to the end of the question. It is also very rare nowadays to use *whom* with a preposition.

  *Who did you go the conference **with**?* (NOT ~~With whom did you go to the conference?~~)

  *Which address did you send it **to**?* (NOT ~~To which address did you send it?~~)

  *What do you base your theory **on**?* (NOT ~~On what do you base your theory?~~)

Exercises

17.1 Underline the correct words.

1   What *did you talk about/you talked about* in your presentation?
2   How *works a hybrid car/does a hybrid car work*?
3   How much profit did *Berkshire Hathaway make/Berkshire Hathaway made*?
4   Why *Ford's market share is falling/is Ford's market share falling*?
5   *What Vice-President/Which Vice-President* is chairing the meeting?
6   *What advice/Which advice* did she give you about your career?
7   *To who is this bag/Whose bag is this*?
8   *What type of loan are you interested in/In what type of loan are you interested*?

17.2 Expand the *And you?* questions to make full questions.

1   I get to work around 8.30. And you?   When _____*do you get to work?*_____
2   I'm staying at the Sheraton. And you?   Where _____
3   I paid €150 for the flight. And you?   How much _____
4   I've interviewed three candidates. And you? How many candidates _____
5   I've been waiting for an hour. And you?   How long _____
6   I'll have the steak. And you?   What _____

17.3 Complete the questions about the rail company Thalys with these phrases: *How big, How far, How fast, How long, How many, How often*.

1   ____*How many*____ passengers does Thalys transport per year?
2   _____ is Thalys, in terms of turnover and number of employees?
3   _____ do Thalys trains leave Paris Gare du Nord for Brussels?
4   _____ is Brussels from Paris?
5   _____ does the journey take?
6   _____ does a Thalys train travel – what's the maximum speed?

17.4 In this dialogue from a job interview, the following words are missing: *are, did, do, have* (x2), *is*. Put them back in the right place.

A: Could I just check what your name?   B: Of course, it's Alison Tucker.
A: So, Alison, what you doing at the moment?   B: I'm working as an administrator.
A: I see. What you do before that?   B: I was a secretary in a law firm.
A: How long you been in your present job?   B: Oh, about four years.
A: What kind of responsibilities you had?   B: Basically, I run the whole office.
A: And why you want to leave?   B: I want to develop my career.

A Subject/object questions

- Compare:

Subject question	Object question
A: **Who** called? B: **Susie** called.	A: **Who** did Susie call? B: Susie called **Mike**.
A: **What** caused the explosion? B: **A gas leak** caused the explosion.	A: **What** did the explosion cause? B: It caused **the factory to close** for a week.
Who and *What* are the **subjects** of the question. They refer to *Susie* and *a gas leak*, the subjects of the reply.	*Who* and *What* are the **objects** of the question. They refer to *Mike* and *the factory*, the objects of the reply.

Start by identifying your target customer. For example, if you sell financial planning, focus on retirement or paying for college. **Who needs** those things? Similarly, **who do you know** who knows someone else who needs those things?

Business Week website

- Notice that we make the questions on the left without *do/does/did*. So:

  (NOT ~~Who did call?~~ → **Susie** called.)

  (NOT ~~What did cause the explosion?~~ → **A gas leak** caused the explosion.)

- Here are more examples of subject/object questions.

Subject question	Object question
Who is going to help you?	**Who** are you going to help?
What has done this?	**What** have you done?
Whose car is blocking the exit?	**Whose car** is that motorbike blocking?
How many people were complaining?	**How many people** were you speaking to?

B Indirect questions

I have a painting by Gerald J. Burns. **Could you tell me** where I can find out the value?

Dallas Arts Revue website

- We can be more polite by beginning a question with an indirect phrase like:

  Could you tell me ... ?
  Do you know ... ?
  Could I just check ...?

- The form of an indirect question is like an affirmative statement, not like a direct question. Compare:

  direct   *Where **is the station**?*
  indirect   *Could you tell me where **the station is**?*   (NOT ~~where is the station~~)
  direct   *When **does the talk start**?*
  indirect   *Do you know when **the talk starts**?*   (NOT ~~when does the talk start~~)
  direct   *What **is the price**?*
  indirect   *Could I just check what **the price is**?*   (NOT ~~what is the price~~)

- *Yes/no* indirect questions use *if*. The form is also like an affirmative statement.

  direct   ***Is this** the right room for the marketing seminar?*
  indirect   *Do you know **if this is** the right room for the marketing seminar?*

Exercises

18.1 <u>Underline</u> the correct words.

1   Who *did meet you/<u>met you</u>* at the airport?
2   Who *did you meet/you met* at the airport?
3   Who *started Microsoft/did start Microsoft*?
4   When *started Microsoft/did Microsoft start*?
5   Who *did speak/spoke* at the conference?
6   What *did she speak/she spoke* about?
7   What *did happen/happened*?
8   Why *did it happen/it happened*?
9   Who *told you/did tell you*?
10 Who *you told/did you tell*?

18.2 Match questions 1–10 above with answers a)–j) below.

1 ☐ *b*   2 ☐   3 ☐   4 ☐   5 ☐   6 ☐   7 ☐   8 ☐   9 ☐   10 ☐

a) I met Mrs Chang.
b) Mrs Chang met me.
c) It started in 1975.
d) Bill Gates started it.
e) Linda spoke.

f) She spoke about nanotechnology.
g) It happened because of bad management.
h) Nothing happened.
i) I told my line manager immediately.
j) My line manager told me.

23 **18.3** The CEO of a large company is giving a press conference. Sometimes what he says is not very clear. Complete the journalists' questions.

CEO	**Journalists**
1 We made a profit last year.	Sorry? How much profit __*did you make?*__
2 One division made 50% of the total.	Excuse me? Which division __*made 50% of the total?*__
3 We launched several new models.	OK, but how many models _____
4 One model now has 6% market share.	Really? Which model _____
5 But one Board member resigned.	Really? Who _____
6 Half a million euros went missing.	Sorry? How much money _____
7 He used his wife's bank account.	What? Whose bank account _____
8 The police found him in Panama.	Excuse me? Where _____

24 **18.4** A passenger is travelling by train. Rewrite each question, beginning as shown.

1   Where is the ticket office?   Do you know __*where the ticket office is?*__
2   How much does the ticket cost?   Could you tell me _____
3   When does the train leave?   Do you know _____
4   Which platform is it?   Could I just check _____
5   Do I have to change trains?   Could you tell me _____
6   Am I in the right seat?   Do you know _____

19 Time expressions 1

A Time in relation to today

- We say:

  the day before yesterday/yesterday/today/tomorrow/the day after tomorrow.

- We say:

  the week before last/last week/this week/next week/the week after next.

- And for parts of yesterday, today and tomorrow we say:

yesterday	*yesterday morning/yesterday afternoon/last night.*
today	*this morning/this afternoon/this evening/tonight.*
tomorrow	*tomorrow morning/tomorrow afternoon/tomorrow night.*

B Calendar references

- Compare the UK and USA:

	UK	**USA**
saying a date	*the seventh of April* or *April the seventh*	*April seven*
writing a date	*7 April* or *7th April* or *April 7th*	*April 7*
writing a full date	day/month/year: *7/4/06*	month/day/year: *4/7/06*

C *In/on/at*, no preposition

- We say:

in	*in the morning/in June/in the summer/in the third quarter/in 2004/ in the 21st century.*
on	*on Friday/on Friday morning/on the 28th of July/on my birthday/ on Christmas Day.*
at	*at 4.30/at midday/at the weekend/at the end of the week/at night/ at Christmas.*
no preposition	*yesterday/this week/last week/next week/a few days ago/ yesterday afternoon/tomorrow morning/the day before yesterday.*

- We can use *in* to talk about 'time from now'.

  *We're going to launch the new line of products **in** two weeks.*

D Time adverbs from previous units

- Check units 1, 2, 4, 5, 7 to see which time adverbs go with which verb forms.

present simple	*always, sometimes, daily, every week, from time to time, etc.*
present continuous	*at the moment, this week, nowadays, currently, right now, etc.*
past simple	*in 2004, in the nineties, a few days ago, last year, etc.*
past continuous	*when, while.*
present perfect	*ever, never, already, not yet, for, since, this year, up to now, etc.*

- Some frequency adverbs like *always, often, never* can be used with the present simple or the present perfect.

Exercises

19.1 It is now Wednesday lunchtime. Put phrases a)–j)
into time order, with 1 as the most distant in
the past and 10 as the most distant in the future.

a) this evening

b) last night

c) tonight

d) this afternoon

e) this morning

f) yesterday morning

g) the day after tomorrow

h) the week before last

i) tomorrow afternoon

j) the day before yesterday

*The Night Before the Big Meeting Frank Receives a
Visit from the PowerPoint Fairy.*

1 ⟦h⟧   2 ☐   3 ☐   4 ☐   5 ☐   **NOW**   6 ☐   7 ☐   8 ☐   9 ☐   10 ☐

19.2 After each example, write *UK* for British usage or *USA* for American usage.

Spoken

1 'the twenty-eighth of July' _____

2 'July twenty-eight' _____

3 'July the twenty-eighth' _____

Written

4 (Christmas Day) December 25 _____

5 (Christmas Day 2007) 25/12/07 _____

6 (Christmas Day 2007) 12/25/07 _____

Now write your own birthday like in example 5 and 6.

British style: ___ / ___ / ___   American style: ___ / ___ / ___

19.3 Put *in, on* or *at*.

1 _at_ + clock times (*10.00*)

2 _____ + season (*the winter*)

3 _____ + year (*2005*)

4 _____ + day (*Thursday*)

5 _____ + date (*12 March*)

6 _____ + month (*March*)

7 _____ + part of the day (*the evening*)

8 _____ + day + part of day (*Monday morning*)

9 _____ + holiday periods (*Easter*)

10 _____ + single holiday days (*Easter Sunday*)

11 _____ + special days (*my birthday*)

12 _____ + *the weekend/the end of the year*

19.4 Write these adverbs in the column where they are used most often: ~~ago~~, *already, at the moment, currently, every week, last week, not yet, nowadays, once a year, since, so far this year, these days, up to now, usually, yesterday.*

Present simple (I work)	Present continuous (I am working)	Past simple (I worked)	Present perfect (I have worked)
		ago	

20 Time expressions 2

A For/since/during/ago

- We use *for* and *since* with the present perfect to talk about time. *For* refers to a period of time and *since* refers to when it started.

  *I've worked here **for two years**.* (period of time)
  *I've worked here **since 2004**.* (point in time when something started)

- We can use *for* with other tenses.

  *I'm going to/I went to Stockholm **for** a few days.*

- We can also use *during* to talk about periods of time. *During* answers the question 'when?'. *For* answers the question 'how long?'.

  *I didn't feel nervous **during** my presentation.* (when?)
  *The presentation lasted **for** about an hour.* (how long?)

- *Ago* means 'before the present'. We use it with the past simple.

  *I started working here two years **ago**.* (NOT ~~since two years~~)

B Actually ≠ now

- The word *actually* does not mean 'now'. It means 'in fact' or 'really'. This is a common mistake.

- Words that mean 'now' include: *at the present time, currently, nowadays, these days.*

  ***Nowadays** companies are thinking much more about the environment.*

C On time/in time

- *On time* means 'at the right time'. *In time* means 'with enough time'.

  *The plane took off **on time**.* (not early and not late)
  *We arrived at the airport **in time** to have a meal.* (early enough to do something)

D By/until

- *By* means 'on or before'. *Until* means 'up to'.

  *I need your report **by Friday**.* (on or before Friday – perhaps Thursday)
  *I'll be away **until Friday**.* (up to and including Friday)

E At the end/in the end/at last

- *At the end* refers to the last part of something. *In the end* means 'eventually' or 'finally'.

  ***At the end** of the product demonstration she gave us some samples.*
  *We waited for nearly an hour, and **in the end** we left.*

- *At last* shows pleasure because something happens that you have been waiting for.

  ***At last** we've completed all the tests on the new drug – now we can start selling it.*

Exercises

20.1 <u>Underline</u> the correct words.

1 We've been in the asset management business *for*/*during* ten years.

2 We moved into the asset management business *for*/*during* the 1990s.

3 This machine was serviced *since three months*/*three months ago*.

4 This machine hasn't been serviced *since January*/*for January*.

5 This machine hasn't been serviced *since three months*/*for three months*.

6 We used to take orders over the phone, but *actually*/*nowadays* we do it online.

20.2 Complete this email using: *ago, for, in, nowadays, since*. (See unit 19 for *in*.)

Subject	application for job LON386

I saw your advertisement on the JobSeekers website a few days (1) _____ , and
I would like to apply for job ref LON386, which is to work as an accountant in London. You will
see from my attached CV that I have been working as a trainee accountant here in Milan
(2) _____ six months, (3) _____ leaving university. I would like to work
abroad to develop my career as I know that (4) _____ companies are looking for
international experience. I will call you (5) _____ a few days to check you have
received my application.

20.3 <u>Underline</u> the correct words.

1 We have to finish this project *by*/*until* the end of the week.

2 If you arrive *on time*/*in time*, we can talk before the meeting starts.

3 It's important to arrive at meetings *on time*/*in time* in Switzerland.

4 I waited at your office *by*/*until* one o'clock, and then I left.

5 I'll be at your office *by*/*until* one o'clock – perhaps even earlier.

25 **20.4** Complete the dialogue using these words: *at last, by, until, on time, in time*.

MARIA: Where is Nicola? The plane leaves at 11.00, and Emirates flights are nearly always
(1) _____ . If she doesn't get here (2) _____ about 10.15, she's going to
miss it.

FREDERIK: Perhaps we can wait a little longer.

MARIA: No, let's go to the departure gate now – I want to be (3) _____ to get a free
newspaper. The last time I flew with Emirates there weren't any left.

FREDERIK: Oh, look, there's Nicola! (4) _____ she's arrived!

NICOLA: Hi everyone! Sorry I'm late. I was at a party (5) _____ midnight and I didn't hear my
alarm clock this morning. I hope you haven't been worrying.

21 Passive 1

A Form

● We form the passive with *be* + the past participle.

Active	Passive
Currency dealers **trade** millions of dollars every day.	Millions of dollars **are traded** every day.
Mike **is installing** the software tomorrow.	The software **is being installed** tomorrow.
The Central Bank **raised** interest rates by 0.25%.	Interest rates **were raised** by 0.25%.
They **have chosen** Mr Brady as the new CEO.	Mr Brady **has been chosen** as the new CEO.
We **will make** a decision tomorrow.	A decision **will be made** tomorrow.
Someone **should clean** this machine every month.	This machine **should be cleaned** every month.

● When people or things do an action, we use the active form of the verb (*trade, raised,* etc).

When we say how people or things are affected by an action – what happens to them – we use the passive form of the verb (*are traded, were raised,* etc).

B Uses

● **Use 1**

We use the passive when the person or organization who does the action is obvious, unimportant or unknown. The examples in section A show this.

*Millions of dollars **are traded** every day.* (who does the trading is obvious)
*The software **is being installed** tomorrow.* (who does the installing is unimportant)
*This machine **should be cleaned** every month.* (who does the cleaning is unknown)

● **Use 2**

We often use the passive at the beginning of a sentence to refer back to something that was just mentioned.

DreamWorks *is one of Hollywood's most successful studios.* It *was started by Steven Spielberg in 1994.*

Using the active in the second sentence would sound strange – the sentence would not follow so well.

*DreamWorks is one of Hollywood's most successful studios. ~~Steven Spielberg~~ **started it in 1994**.*

C Saying who does the action: *by*

● If we want to say who does the action in a passive sentence we use *by*.

*DreamWorks was started **by Steven Spielberg**.*
*Millions of dollars are traded **by currency dealers** every day.*

But in many cases using *by* sounds strange and unnecessary.

A decision will be made ~~by us~~ tomorrow. (Why mention *by us*?)
I was shown round the factory ~~by someone~~ after lunch. (Why mention *by someone*?)

Exercises

21.1 Cross out the error in each sentence. Write the correction at the end.

1   These TV screens are ~~making~~ in Korea.   *made*
2   Our factory was been closed for a week because of a strike.
3   India's infrastructure is be modernized very rapidly.
4   This line was create by one of our best young designers.
5   Your invoice will being paid next week.
6   The assembly is doing mostly by industrial robots.

21.2 Rewrite each sentence with a passive verb, without mentioning who does the action.

1   China imports most of its soy beans from Brazil.
    Most of China's soy beans __*are imported*__ from Brazil.
2   We are reorganizing our customer services department.
    Our customer services department _____
3   Steve Jobs founded Apple Computers in 1976.
    Apple Computers _____ in 1976.
4   The slow progress in our Latin American markets has disappointed us.
    We _____ by the slow progress in our Latin American markets.

21.3 Cross out the phrases which are not necessary. If every phrase is necessary put a tick (✓).

1   This machine was repaired ~~by a technician~~ yesterday.
2   This machine was repaired by the technician with the long hair and glasses. ✓
3   English is spoken all over the world by people.
4   You will be met at the airport by someone holding a sign with your name on it.
5   You will be met at the airport by someone and taken to your hotel.

26 **21.4** Put the first two verbs into the present simple passive (*is/are done*) and the second two into the present continuous passive (*is/are being done*).

From mass marketing to micro marketing

The mass market is disappearing. These days, even detergent brands (1) _____ (target) at particular market segments. The days of selling to anonymous crowds of people are gone – now every customer (2) _____ (see) as an individual. This evolution from mass to micro marketing (3) _____ (cause) by changes in society. Cultures are becoming more diverse and customers want a product that is 'right for me'. At the same time, mass media like network television channels (4) _____ (replace) by hundreds of other communication channels like computer terminals, cell phone screens, and specialized magazines. For marketing departments, life is going to get interesting.

A Formal contexts

- With the passive we often do not mention who or what does the action. (See unit 21.) This produces a formal, impersonal style that is typical of business reports, legal contracts or written complaints.

  *The package you sent **was received** at this office yesterday. When we opened it we found that the goods **were damaged**. These items **are needed** urgently and so we request that you send a replacement order immediately.*

B Systems and processes

One excellent example of a complicated supply chain is the auto manufacturing industry. In some cases, raw materials **may be sourced** from Asia, **assembled** into components in Mexico, **shipped** back to Asia for further assembly, and then **sent** to Poland to be assembled into the vehicle.

World Trade Magazine website

- The passive is often used to describe systems and processes. It focuses on the action (the verb).

  *When a privately owned company issues shares of stock to the general public it **is called** an Initial Public Offering (IPO). The process is complicated, and months of planning **are involved**. <u>First</u>, a board of directors **is assembled** and accounts **are audited** for accuracy. <u>Then</u>, the company appoints an investment bank to act as underwriter. Underwriters have the business contacts to offer the company's shares to the right investors. The initial offering price of the share **is** also **set** by them.*

- To show a sequence in a process we can use linking words like: *first/first of all, then, the next step, next, after that, finally*. Two are <u>underlined</u> above.

C Balance of active and passive

- Find a balance of active and passive forms. Using too many passive forms makes a text difficult to read.
  - Look at the example above about damaged goods. The passive forms are in **bold**, but the following are all active: *sent, opened, found, request, send*.
  - Look at the example about IPOs. The passive forms are in **bold**, but the following are all active: *issues, is, appoints, have*.

D Passive + infinitive

The average selling price of DVD recorders **is expected to fall** by as much as 50 percent later this year as Taiwanese shipments of DVD recorders increase sharply.

PC World website

- The verbs *believe, expect, know, predict, say, suppose, think* are often used in the passive followed by an infinitive (*to do/to be*). This is common in written reports where we want to make our language less certain.

  *The economy **is expected to grow** next year by around 2%.*
  *Our profits **are predicted to fall** slightly in the next quarter.*
  *Our Ljubljana office **is supposed to open** next spring.*
  *The board of directors **is thought to favour** a merger with another bank.*

E *To be born*

- Note the passive form *to be born*: *I **was born** in 1987.*

Exercises

22.1 Rewrite each sentence with a passive verb. This exercise includes revision of unit 21.

1 Customers in all our target markets will see this advert.

This advert _____*will be seen*_____ by customers in all our target markets.

2 Someone gave me a copy of the report.

I _____ a copy of the report.

3 Chris gave me a copy of the report.

I _____ Chris.

4 People expect that the price of oil will rise over the winter period.

The price of oil _____ over the winter period.

5 People think that bonds are a safer investment than shares.

Bonds _____ a safer investment than shares.

6 Geneva is my place of birth.

I _____ in Geneva.

27 **22.2** Put the verbs into the present simple active or passive.

How to make an espresso

First, you (1) _____*need*_____ (need) good quality beans.
Then, the beans (2) ___*are ground*___ (grind) very finely into
a powder. Next, the ground beans (3) _____ (place)
into a container in the espresso machine. The base of the machine
(4) _____ (contain) water, and when you (5) _____ (heat) the water,
it boils and turns into steam. The steam (6) _____ (force) through the coffee
by the funnel shape of the container. Finally, the steam condenses at the top of the machine
and the liquid (7) _____ (fall) back into a container. Machines in daily use
(8) _____ (should/clean) regularly to keep the fresh coffee taste.

22.3 <u>Underline</u> four linking words in the 'espresso' text above used to show a sequence.

28 **22.4** The text on the left needs to be changed to make it more formal. Rewrite it using the same verbs in the correct form of the passive.

Employment contract

If an employee thinks someone <u>has treated</u> them unfairly, they <u>should refer</u> the matter to their line manager. The line manager will arrange a meeting, which he or she <u>must schedule</u> within two weeks. You <u>can invite</u> a trade union representative to the meeting.

EMPLOYMENT CONTRACT

If an employee thinks they (1) _____
unfairly, the matter (2) _____ to
their line manager. The line manager will arrange a meeting, which
(3) _____ within two weeks. A trade
union representative (4) _____ to
the meeting.

23 Modal verbs 1: ability and requests

"Miss Dugan, will you send someone in here who can distinguish right from wrong?"

A Introduction

- Modal verbs are auxiliary verbs – they are used with another main verb. Modal verbs are *can, could, will, would, must, may, might, shall* and *should*.
- Two modal verbs cannot be put together. (NOT ~~I can will meet you~~)
- Modal verbs are followed by the infinitive without *to*. (NOT ~~I must to meet him~~)
- Modal verbs have only one form, so there is no third person *-s* and no *-ing, -ed*.
- To make a question we put the modal in front of the subject. To make a negative we put *not* after the modal (often shortened to *-n't*).

Can I ...?	*I cannot (can't)*	*May I ...?*	*I may not*
Could I ...?	*I could not (couldn't)*	*Might I ...?*	*I might not*
Will I ...?	*I will not (won't)*	*Shall I ...?*	*I shall not (shan't)*
Would I ...?	*I would not (wouldn't)*	*Should I ...?*	*I should not (shouldn't)*
Must I ...?	*I must not (mustn't)*		

- Modal verbs are used to express ideas such as ability, obligation, probability. The same modal verb can have different meanings.

B Ability

- To talk about ability we use *can* and *can't* (or *could/couldn't* in the past).

  *I **can** understand English, but I **can't** express my opinion very well in meetings.*
  *I **couldn't** open your email attachment – please send it again.*

- We sometimes use *be able to* instead of *can*. *Be able to* forms tenses.

  *From next week customers **will be able to** access our online help service.*

C Requests and permission

- To request that someone else does something, we use *can/could* and *will/would*.

  ***Can/Will** you give me a hand?*
  ***Could/Would** you wait here, please?* (*could/would* are formal and polite)

- To request something for ourselves (permission) we use *can/could* and *may*.

  *The battery on my mobile phone is dead – **can** I use your recharger?*
  ***May** I come in?* (*may* is formal and polite)

D Suggestions

- To make a suggestion we use *Shall I* and *Shall we*.

  ***Shall I** open a window?*
  ***Shall we** have a break for coffee now?*

- There are other phrases to make suggestions. Notice the forms of *have* below.

  ***Let's/Why don't we** <u>have</u> a break?*
  ***How about/What about** <u>having</u> a break?*

Exercises

23.1 <u>Underline</u> the correct words.

1 *Do you come/<u>Can you come</u>* to the meeting next week?

2 *I can come/I can to come* to the meeting next week.

3 *I don't can come/I can't come* to the meeting next week.

4 I missed the last meeting, but *I will can/I will be able to* come to the next one.

5 Sorry that *I couldn't/I didn't could* come to the meeting last week.

6 Sorry that *I wasn't able to/I wasn't able* come to the meeting last week.

7 When *we can have/can we have* the next meeting?

8 Shall *we meet/we to meet* again next week?

9 How about *meeting/we meet* again next week?

10 *May you/Could you* help me?

23.2 Rewrite the sentence on the left in a more polite way using *could, would* or *may*. There are two answers each time.

1 Can you wait for me?   *Could you wait for me?* and _____

2 Can I ask who is calling? _____ and _____

3 Can you repeat that?   _____ and _____

4 Can I interrupt you?   _____ and _____

23.3 Rewrite these suggestions.

1 Would you like me to call a taxi?

2 Let's go to that new Italian restaurant.

3 Why don't we go for a drink after work?

4 Do you want me to call back tomorrow?

Shall _____*I call a taxi?*_____

Shall _____

Shall _____

Shall _____

23.4 Complete the conversation between a flight attendant and a passenger. Each time use *would, may* or *shall* as the first word + *I* or *you* as the second word.

ATTENDANT: Excuse me, madam, we're going to take off in a moment. (1) __*Would*__ ___*you*___ push your bag under the seat in front?

PASSENGER: Yes, of course, but there isn't much room.

ATTENDANT: (2) _____ _____ see if there's any space in a locker at the back of the plane?

PASSENGER: Thanks, that would be better. And (3) _____ _____ have a pillow and blanket after take off? I'm really tired.

ATTENDANT: Of course, madam.

PASSENGER: Oh yes – (4) _____ _____ bring me an eye mask as well? Thank you so much.

"It's not enough that we succeed. Cats must also fail."

A Obligation (it's necessary to do it)

- 'Obligation' means something is necessary. We use *must* and *have to*.

  I **must/have to** *finish this report before I go home.*

- *Must* and *have to* are very similar, but there can be a small difference. *You must* sounds like the speaker personally feels it is important. *You have to* sounds like the situation makes it necessary.

  You **must** *try to relax – all this stress is no good for you.*   (I'm telling you)
  You **have to** *go outside the building if you want to smoke.*   (the rules say so)

- For written orders and instructions *must* is normally used.

  Passengers **must** *remove their coats before passing through the X-ray machine.*

- In everyday speech we can use *have got to* or *need to* instead of *have to*.

  I'm busy this afternoon – I **'ve got to** *prepare my presentation.*

B No obligation (it's not necessary to do it)

- 'No obligation' means that something is not necessary – there is a choice. We use *don't have to* or *don't need to*. Note that *mustn't* is not used with this meaning.

  You **don't have to** *decide now – think about it and I'll call you tomorrow.*

C Permission (it's OK to do it)

- 'Permission' means that you are allowed to do something. We use *can*.

  You **can** *smoke in part of the staff canteen, but not in the rest of the building.*

D Prohibition (don't do it)

- 'Prohibition' means that you are not allowed to do something – it is forbidden. We use *mustn't* and *can't*.

  Passengers **mustn't** *leave their bags unattended.*   (it's an order: we're telling you)
  I'm sorry, but you **can't** *park there.*   (it's impossible: the rules say so)

E Opinions and advice (it's a good thing to do)

- We use *should/shouldn't* to give an opinion about what is a good/bad thing to do.

  I think we **should** *spend more money on research and development.*

- When we speak to another person our opinion (*you should*) becomes advice.

  I think **you should** *start looking for another job if you're not happy.*

- Notice that *should* is like a weak form of *must/have to*.

  You **should** *speak to the HR Director.*   (advice: it's the best thing to do)

  You **must/have to** *speak to the HR Director.*   (strong advice: it's really necessary)

> You **don't have to** answer the phone. What's wrong with letting voicemail take a message? I think it's insulting to interrupt a meeting to take an incoming call.
>
> **Succeeding in Business website**

> When preparing for an interview, most applicants concentrate on formulating answers to potential questions. However, it is just as important to prepare a few good questions they **should** ask during the interview.
>
> **CNN website**

Exercises

24.1 <u>Underline</u> the correct words so that a) and b) have the same meaning.

1 a) I think it's a good idea for us to redesign the packaging.

b) I think we *have to/should/can't* redesign the packaging.

2 a) It's not necessary for you to wait for me.

b) You *mustn't/have to/don't have to* wait for me.

3 a) It's necessary for me to speak to my boss before I can agree to this.

b) I *have to/can't/shouldn't* speak to my boss before I can agree to this.

4 a) It's a bad idea for us to increase our prices this year.

b) We *can't/shouldn't/don't have to* increase our prices this year.

5 a) I'm not allowed to give you a discount – it's against company policy.

b) I *should/don't have to/can't* give you a discount – it's against company policy.

6 a) Don't tell anyone about my new job.

b) You *mustn't/don't have to/have to* tell anyone about my new job.

24.2 Fill in the gaps with the best word from this list: *must, mustn't, have to, don't have to*.

1 You _____ do it.   = You have a choice. It's not necessary.

2 You _____ do that!   = Don't do that! It's an order.

3 You _____ do it.   = I'm telling you to do it. It's necessary.

4 You _____ do it.   = The rules say to do it. It's necessary.

Now do the same for these words: *can, can't, should, shouldn't*.

5 You _____ do it.   = It's a good thing to do. It's my advice.

6 You _____ do it.   = It's a bad thing to do. It's my advice.

7 You _____ do it.   = It's OK to do it. It's allowed.

8 You _____ do that.   = It's impossible to do it. The rules say so.

30 **24.3** Complete this meeting extract using: *can, can't, need to, don't have to*.

The final item on the agenda is 'Procedure for holidays'. There was a lot of confusion in July and August when everyone wanted to take holidays at the same time, so I (1) _____ explain this clearly. The most important thing is to give our Human Resources Manager, Sandra, as much notice as possible – you (2) _____ go on holiday unless you have told her at least four weeks in advance. Also, some people seem to think that it's necessary to take all their holiday time before the end of the calendar year. That's not true – you (3) _____ if you want to, but you (4) _____ . If you have some days remaining, you can carry them forward to the next year. I hope that's clear now – I don't want the same thing to happen next summer.

25 Modal verbs 3: probability

A Certainty

- We use *will* and *won't* when we are certain about something in the future.

  *Our next generation of vehicles **will** use fuel cell technology.*
  *I'm sorry, I **won't** be in the office on that day.*

- To make *will* and *won't* less certain we can use words like *I think* and *probably*. (See unit 12.)

B Deduction

- We use *must* and *can't* for deduction. This is when we decide that something is true because it is logical from the information we have and nothing else seems possible.

  *There's no answer from her phone – she **must** be in a meeting.*
  *That **can't** be Diana over there – she's in Portugal on holiday.* (NOT ~~mustn't~~)

C Expectation

- We use *should* and *shouldn't* when we expect that something will/will not happen.

  *They **should** arrive here at about nine thirty.*
  *That **shouldn't** be a problem.*

D Uncertainty

- We use *may*, *might* and *could* for things that are possible. This is like 'perhaps' or 'the probability is 50/50'.

  *We **may** have to increase our prices next year.* (= perhaps we will)
  *Unemployment **could** start to rise before the election.* (= perhaps it will)

- There is no difference between *may*, *might* and *could* for this meaning.

- The negative forms are *may not* and *might not*. Note that *could not* is not used with this meaning.

  *I **may not** be back in the office until tomorrow – can you take any messages for me?*
  (NOT ~~I could not be back in the office until tomorrow~~)

E Degrees of probability

- The modals above show different degrees of probability.

100%	certainty	will, won't	*That **will** be Janet at the door.*
90 – 100%	deduction	must, can't	*You **must** be tired after your journey.*
70 – 90%	expectation	should, shouldn't	*Come with us – it **should** be fun.*
30 – 70%	uncertainty	may, might, could	*Don't wait for me – I **might** be late.*

"This might not be ethical. Is that a problem for anybody?"

Exercises

25.1 Choose the best way a)–c) to continue each sentence.

1 He must be out of the office. ☐
2 He might be out of the office. ☐
3 He can't be out of the office. ☐

a) I saw him at the photocopier a moment ago.
b) I've looked everywhere but he's not here.
c) I'll just go and check with his secretary.

25.2 <u>Underline</u> the correct words.

1 Congratulations on your promotion! You *may be/<u>must be</u>* very pleased!
2 I've no idea where she saved the document. It *could be/will be* anywhere.
3 The 29th is a possibility. I *might be/must be* free after lunch.
4 I'll do it now. I *may not have/could not have* time this afternoon.
5 There's someone waiting for you in reception. It *can be/could be* Ms Kumar.
6 There are more and more clouds. I think it *might rain/must rain*.
7 That *can't be/may not be* Soraya. She's away at a conference today.
8 Import prices look stable – they *couldn't rise/shouldn't rise* too much this year.
9 Lisa isn't usually late. She *should be/must be* stuck in the traffic.
10 Sorry, I'm very busy – I *shouldn't come/may not come* to your presentation.
11 A: 'They want to renegotiate the contract!' B: 'You *should be/must be* joking.'
12 A: 'They want to renegotiate the contract!' B: 'You *can't be/may not be* serious.'

31 **25.3** Complete the mini-dialogues with these words: *could not, may, might not, must, mustn't, won't*. Note that two are not used.

1 A: These figures could be wrong. B: Yes, that's possible. They _____ be.
2 A: These figures can't be right. B: Yes, I agree. They _____ be wrong.
3 A: These figures may not be right. B: Yes, I agree. They _____ be.
4 A: There shouldn't be any problem. B: Yes, I agree. There probably _____ be.

32 **25.4** During a conference coffee break two colleagues are discussing another delegate. Complete their dialogue using: *can't be, might be, must be, shouldn't be*.

ELENA: Who is that man over there with the pink tie? Is it Jacques?

MANUEL: I'm not sure. It (1) _____ . But I always thought that Jacques was older.

ELENA: Yes, I think you're right. But if it's not Jacques, then it (2) _____ Remy.

MANUEL: No, that's impossible. It (3) _____ Remy. Remy is a lot shorter.

ELENA: Oh, I know who it is. It's Philippe. I'd like to speak to him at some point.

MANUEL: OK, that (4) _____ difficult. Let's go and introduce ourselves right now.

26 Modal verbs 4: modals in the past

A Ability in the past (it was possible/impossible)

- For ability in the present we use *can* and *can't*. (See unit 23.)
- To talk about ability in the past we use *could, couldn't, was able to* and *wasn't able to*.

  *I **could** speak French when I was at school, but now I've forgotten most of it.*
  *I **was able to** speak French quite well when I was at school.*

- To talk about one specific past action we only use *was able to*.

  *When I went to their offices I **was able to** meet the sales director.* (NOT ~~I could meet~~)

B Obligation in the past (it was necessary/not necessary)

- For obligation in the present we use *must* and *have to*. (See unit 24.)
- To talk about obligation in the past we use *had to* and *didn't have to*. There is no past form of *must*.

  *In my last job we **had to** get a doctor's note if we were ill for more than two days.*

C Opinions and advice in the past (it was a good/bad idea)

- For opinions and advice in the present we use *should* and *shouldn't*. (See unit 24.)
- To talk about opinions and advice in the past we use *should/shouldn't* + *have* + past participle.

  *I think you **should have spoken** to your boss before you signed the contract.*
  *Are you feeling ill? You **shouldn't have eaten** so much!*

D Probability in the past (it was certain/uncertain)

- For different degrees of probability in the present/future see the table in unit 25 section E.
- For the past we use the same modals + *have* + past participle. So, for example:

certainty	*We're a few minutes early. The talk **won't have started** yet.*
deduction	*Surely I **can't have lost** my passport. I **must have left** it at the hotel.*
expectation	*They **should have arrived** by now. I wonder where they are?*
uncertainty	*Can you check the invoice? I think you **may have made** a mistake.*
uncertainty	*We're only a few minutes late. The talk **might not have** started yet.*

- For uncertainty we use the affirmative forms *may/might/could have done* and the negative forms *may/might not have done*.

  But notice that the form *could not have done* has a different meaning. It is used for deduction (something is true because it is logical), the same as *can't have done*.

  *Surely I **can't/couldn't have lost** my passport. I had it with me just a moment ago.*

Exercises

26.1 <u>Underline</u> the correct words. Sometimes both choices are correct.

1 When I was a child I *could/was able to* play the piano and the flute.

2 I lost my laptop, but I *could/was able to* borrow another one.

3 In those days the company had more money and we *could/were able to* take our clients to the most expensive restaurants.

4 The traffic was bad, but I *could/was able to* get to their offices on time.

33

26.2 Complete the dialogue with these words: *had to go, didn't have to go, should have gone, shouldn't have gone.*

TOM: The conference was really boring. It was a mistake. I (1) _____

CAROL: So why were you there? Surely you (2) _____

TOM: No, you don't understand. You see I (3) _____ last year, but I didn't. So this year I (4) _____ . My boss insisted.

26.3 Look at situations a)–f). Then match them with sentences 1–6 below. Be careful – some are very similar.

a) Maria did it. I can say this for certain without having any more information.

b) Maria didn't do it. I can say this for certain without having any more information.

c) From the information that I have, it seems logical that Maria did it.

d) From the information that I have, it seems logical that Maria didn't do it.

e) It's possible that Maria did it.

f) It was necessary for Maria to do it.

1 Maria will have done it.   ☐

2 Maria must have done it.   ☐

3 Maria had to do it.   ☐

4 Maria won't have done it.   ☐

5 Maria can't have done it.   ☐

6 Maria might have done it.   ☐

26.4 Rewrite each sentence so that it has the same meaning. Use these phrases: *can't have, could have, might not have, must have, should have.*

1 It was possible for you to call me.   = You _____ called me.

2 I expected the talk to start by now.   = The talk _____ started by now.

3 I'm sure she didn't say that.   = She _____ said that.

4 I'm sure your talk was a success.   = Your talk _____ been a success.

5 Perhaps the letter didn't arrive.   = The letter _____ arrived.

27 Conditionals 1: zero and first conditional

A Conditions and results

- Conditional sentences are explained in units 27–30. Compare:

	Time reference	Name
If sales **go up**, *I* <u>usually</u> **get** *a bonus.*	general	zero conditional
If sales **go up** <u>next month</u>, *I'll* **get** *a bonus.*	future: likely	first conditional
If sales **went up** <u>next month</u>, *I'd* **get** *a bonus.*	future: unlikely	second conditional
If sales **had gone up** <u>last month</u>, *I'd* **have got** *a bonus.*	past	third conditional

- The *if …* part of the sentence is the condition, and the other part of the sentence is the result. The condition can come second.

  I'll **get** *a bonus if sales* **go up**.
  I'd **get** *a bonus if sales* **went up**.

  Note that there is no comma in writing if the condition comes second.

B Zero conditional

- The form of a zero conditional is:

Condition	Result
- present simple or present continuous	- present simple or imperative
If you **fly** *first class,*	*you* **get** *amazing service.*
If business **is going** *well,*	*everyone* **is** *happy.*
If the lift **isn't working**,	**take** *the stairs.*

- We use a zero conditional to talk about things that are always or generally true. In this type of conditional we are not referring to one specific event.

- In a zero conditional, *if* is the same as *whenever* or *every time*.

  If/whenever/every time interest rates rise, we pay more for our bank loans.

C First conditional

- The form of a first conditional is:

Condition	Result
- present simple or present continuous	- *will/won't* or imperative
If sales **go up** *next month,*	*I'll* **get** *a bonus.*
If you're **leaving** *at six am,*	*I* **won't see** *you in the morning.*
If anyone **calls**,	**say** *I'm in a meeting.*

- We use a first conditional to talk about future events that are likely to happen.

- Note that we do not use *will* in the *if …* part of the sentence.

  (NOT ~~If sales will go up next month, I'll~~ …)

  (NOT ~~If anyone will call, say I'm~~ …)

Exercises

27.1 Complete each sentence 1–6 with the best ending a) or b).

1	If you have any questions,	☐	a)	I deal with them at the end of the talk.
2	Whenever I get questions,	☐	b)	I'll deal with them at the end of my talk.

3	If you wait here,	☐	a)	I'll be right back.
4	If you wait in an airport,	☐	b)	it gets really boring after an hour or so.

5	Whenever I fly Executive Class,	☐	a)	I'll take my laptop with me.
6	If I fly to Sydney next week,	☐	b)	I take my laptop and try to do some work.

27.2 <u>Underline</u> the correct words.

1 If Klaus *speaks/will speak* in a meeting, he usually *mentions/will mention* the importance of our brand image.

2 If Klaus *speaks/will speak* in the meeting tomorrow, I'm sure he *mentions/will mention* the importance of our brand image.

3 Every time *I do/I will do* it, *I make/I will make* the same mistake.

4 It's time to leave. *We are/We'll be* late if *we aren't/we won't be* careful.

5 If *we don't reach/we won't reach* an agreement soon, I think *they walk away/they'll walk away* from the negotiation.

6 Whenever *I use/I will use* this computer, *there's/there'll be* a problem.

7 If *you see/you will see* Nicole, *send her/you will send her* my regards.

8 If *you order/you will order* from our website, we always *send/will send* an email confirmation.

34 **27.3** You are talking to a colleague. Study the first conditional sentences.

> *If I work hard, I'm sure I'll get a promotion after a year. If I get a promotion, I'll have more responsibilities. But … if I have more responsibilities, I won't have so much free time in the evenings. If I don't have so much free time, I won't be able to go to the gym. If I don't go to the gym, I'll get fat. Life isn't easy.*

Now complete what you say in another conversation, using first conditional sentences each time. Use contractions (*'ll* for *will*, etc).

> I've just heard that there might be a strike in the factory. If (1) _____*there's*_____ (there/be) a strike, (2) _____ (we/lose) a lot of production. And if (3) _____ (we/lose) production, (4) _____ (we/not be able) to ship the goods to our customers on time. If (5) _____ (our customers/not be) happy, (6) _____ (they/go) to other suppliers. So it's really important that we negotiate with the unions and try to avoid a strike. If (7) _____ (we/not negotiate) now, I'm sure (8) _____ (there/be) bad labour relations for years to come.

28 Conditionals 2: second conditional

A Second conditional

- The form of a second conditional is:

Condition	Result
- past simple	- would/wouldn't
If I **was** in charge,	I'd **improve** communication in the company.
If we **moved** production to Slovakia,	our costs **wouldn't be** so high.

- We use a second conditional to talk about future events that are imaginary, unlikely or impossible.
- Note that the time reference is the future, even though the past simple is used in the condition.
- Note that we do not use *would* in the *if* … part of the sentence.

   (NOT If I ~~would be~~ in charge)
   (NOT If we ~~would move~~ production)

- Some people say *If I were* … instead of *If I was* … . The *were* form is more formal and is used in the fixed expression *If I were you*.

"If I knew how to get rich quick, would I be sitting on a mountain-top all day?"

B First or second conditional?

- Both the first and second conditionals refer to the future. The choice between them depends on the probability of the event.
- If we think that a future event is likely, we use the first conditional. If we think that a future event is unlikely, imaginary or impossible, we use the second conditional.

   *It'll be a good thing **if** Croatia **joins** the EU.*   (high probability of Croatia joining)
   *It'd be a good thing **if** Morocco **joined** the EU.*   (low probability of Morocco joining)

- The second conditional can sound indirect. It sounds like 'this is just an idea'.

   *If we **order** 1,000 pieces, **will** you give us a discount?*   (direct)
   *If we **ordered** 1,000 pieces, **would** you give us a discount?*   (indirect/imaginary)

C Wishes

- *I wish* is followed by the past simple for general and future wishes. Note how it has the same structure as the second conditional.

   *I **wish** we **had** fewer meetings – I'd have more time to do my work.*
   *If we **had** fewer meetings, I'd have more time to do my work.*

- For wishes concerning ability or possibility we use *I wish I could*.

   *I **wish I could** speak to her, but when I call I just get her voicemail.*

- If the wish is a good one, we use *I hope* + present simple or *will*.

   *I **hope** the negotiations **go** well.*
   *I **hope** the merger **will be** a success.*

Exercises

28.1 <u>Underline</u> the correct words.

1 If America *reduced/would reduce* its trade deficit, the dollar *goes/would go* up.

2 If I *worked/will work* at the EU, I *would support/support* openness and transparency.

3 *I am taking/I'd take* legal advice if *I am/I were* you.

4 I wish that taxes *aren't/weren't* so high.

5 I wish I *can/could* speak better English – life *would/will* be much easier.

6 I hope we *get/could get* many more sales as a result of this advertising campaign.

28.2 Match each sentence 1–6 with its closest context a) or b).

1 I've applied for a new job – if I get it, I'll have to move to London. ☐   a) I have a good chance of getting the job

2 I've applied for a new job – if I got it, I'd have to move to London. ☐   b) I don't think I'll get the job

---

3 If public transport improves, I won't need to drive to work every day. ☐   a) public transport is a very low priority for the government

4 If public transport improved, I wouldn't need to drive to work every day. ☐   b) the government has a plan to improve public transport

---

5 We'd give you a better price if you increased your order. ☐   a) but you don't want to increase your order

6 We'll give you a better price if you increase your order. ☐   b) and I think that you might increase your order

28.3 Complete the conversation by writing each sentence as a second conditional or a wish.

ULRIKE: There's an American-owned company in my field. Sometimes I wonder what it would be like working for them.

ANTONIO: Well, if you (1) _____ (work) for an American company, I suppose your salary (2) _____ (be) better, but perhaps your job (3) _____ (not/be) so secure.

ULRIKE: But, if I (4) _____ (earn) more money, it (5) _____ (not/matter) about the job security!

ANTONIO : Another thing is that the atmosphere in the office might be a lot more competitive. What (6) _____ (happen) if you (7) _____ (not/like) that?

ULRIKE: I don't think it's a question of competition; I think it's about performance. If I (8) _____ (not/work) hard, they (9) _____ (not/keep) me in the company. I understand that – it's called 'hire and fire'. Sometimes I wish we (10) _____ (have) more of that philosophy – it would make our business a lot more efficient.

29 Conditionals 3: more conditional clauses

"The company has a compulsory retirement age of 65 – unless of course you become chairman."

A Unless

- *Unless* means *if not*. It has a first conditional form (present tense in the condition, *will/won't* in the result).

  Unless we **reduce** our costs, we**'ll** go out of business.
  = **If** we **don't reduce** our costs, we**'ll** go out of business.

- We often put the result using *won't* first, and then follow with the condition using *unless*. This gives a strong emphasis.

  *Our supplier **won't** deliver any more parts **unless** we pay all the money we owe them.*

B Provided that/as long as

- We can use *provided that* and *as long as* for emphasis ('if and only if'). They have a first conditional form and the condition usually comes at the end.

  *I **will** sign the contract **provided that** you **guarantee** delivery within ten days.*

- We can use *providing* and *so long as* with the same meaning, but they are more informal.

C In case

- *In case* means 'because something might happen'. It is followed by a present tense with a future time reference (like the condition clause of a first conditional).

  In case I **don't see** you before you leave, have a safe journey back.

- Often the part of the sentence with *in case* comes at the end.

  *I'll take an umbrella **in case** it **rains**.*

D Modal verbs in conditionals

- All modal verbs can be used in conditionals and have their normal meanings. For example, *will/would* mean 'the result is certain' and *can/could* mean 'the result is possible'. Look at these examples.

	'coming in May'	'seeing the factory'
If you **come** in May, you**'ll** see the new factory.	likely	certain, if you come
If you **come** in May, you **can** see the new factory.	likely	possible, if you come
If you **came** in May, you**'d** see the new factory.	unlikely	certain, if you came
If you **came** in May, you **could** see the new factory.	unlikely	possible, if you came

- Here are more examples to show other modal verbs.

  *If he **says** no, you **must try** to persuade him.*
  *If they **ask** you, you **should tell** the truth.*
  *If you **talked** to him personally, he **might change** his mind.*
  *If we **moved** production to Slovakia, our costs **might not be** so high.*

Exercises

29.1 Complete each sentence 1–6 with the best ending a) or b).

1	I'll sign the contract provided that	☐	a)	everyone agrees.
2	I'll sign the contract unless	☐	b)	there's a last-minute problem.

3	The project will be a success as long as	☐	a)	costs get out of control.
4	The project will be a success unless	☐	b)	we keep to the deadlines.

5	The bank will support us provided that	☐	a)	our sales fall dramatically.
6	The bank will support us unless	☐	b)	our business plan is realistic.

29.2 Rewrite the sentences using *unless*.

1 If we don't get a bank loan, we'll have a big cash-flow crisis.

We'll have a big cash-flow crisis *unless we get a bank loan.*

2 Only call me if it's urgent.

Please don't call me _____

3 If they don't offer me a better salary, I won't accept the job.

I won't accept the job _____

4 We'll only finish the project on time if we employ extra staff.

Unless we employ extra staff, we _____

29.3 Join the two sentences together using *in case*.

1 I'll write down your email address. I might forget it.

I'll write down your email address *in case I forget it.*

2 I'm going to save the file on a memory stick. My laptop might stop working.

I'm going to save the file on a memory stick _____

3 I won't confirm the delivery date. Their documents might not be in order.

I won't confirm the delivery date _____

29.4 Look at situations a)–d). Then match them with sentences 1–4.

a) I think the economy won't grow. But if it does, then we'll definitely open an office in Hong Kong.

b) I think the economy won't grow. But if it does, then perhaps we'll open an office in Hong Kong.

c) I think the economy will grow. If it does, then we'll definitely open an office in Hong Kong.

d) I think the economy will grow. If it does, then perhaps we'll open an office in Hong Kong.

1	If the economy continues to grow, we'll open an office in Hong Kong.	☐
2	If the economy continues to grow, we might open an office in Hong Kong.	☐
3	If the economy continued to grow, we'd open an office in Hong Kong.	☐
4	If the economy continued to grow, we might open an office in Hong Kong.	☐

A Third conditional

● The form of a third conditional is:

Condition	Result
- had (not) done	- would (not) have done
If we **had offered** a higher price,	we **wouldn't have got** the contract.

● We use the third conditional to imagine a past action that is the opposite to what really happened. In the example above, this is what really happened:

We offered a low price, and we got the contract.

● Notice that we do not use *would* in the *if …* part of the sentence.

(NOT If we ~~would have offered~~ a higher price, …)

B Affirmatives and negatives

● With the third conditional we are imagining the opposite of what happened. So if what really happened has an affirmative form, the third conditional has a negative form – and vice-versa.

● Look at the affirmative and negative forms.

fact: *You **explained** where the restaurant was. I **found** it.*
but: *If you **hadn't explained** where the restaurant was, I **wouldn't have found** it.*
fact: *You **weren't** at the conference. You **didn't hear** Christine's talk.*
but: *If you **had been** at the conference, you **would have heard** Christine's talk.*

C Contracted forms in speech

● In speech we make contractions. The examples above would sound like this:

*If you **hadn't** explained where the restaurant was, **I wouldn't've** found it.*
*If you**'d** been at the conference, **you'd've** heard Christine's talk.*

D Result in present

● In all the examples above, the imaginary action and its result were both in the past. But often we are thinking about a past action and its result in the present. In this case we use *would (not) do* instead of *would (not) have done*.

fact: *I **ate** the prawns. I **feel** ill. (now)*
but: *If I **hadn't eaten** the prawns, I **wouldn't feel** so ill.*
fact: *I **didn't do** an MBA course. I **don't have** a better job. (now)*
but: *If I **had done** an MBA course, I **would have** a better job.*

Exercises

30.1 <u>Underline</u> the correct words.

1 If you *had told/would have told* me about the problem, I *had done/<u>would have done</u>* something about it.

2 If we *would have known/had known* about their financial problems, we *didn't invest/wouldn't have invested* in the company.

3 If we *had used/would use* magazine adverts instead of street posters, the marketing campaign *would be/would have been* more expensive.

4 We lost the contract. But I think we *would win/would have won* it if we *made/had made* a lower offer.

30.2 Complete the sentence for each situation using a third conditional.

1 fact: Helen didn't get to the airport on time, and so she missed her flight.
   but: If Helen _____*had got*_____ to the airport on time, she _*wouldn't have missed*_ her flight.

2 fact: I didn't know you were coming, so I didn't make a copy of the report.
   but: If I _____ you were coming, I _____ a copy of the report.

3 fact: We booked yesterday, so we got a table at the restaurant.
   but: If we _____ yesterday, we _____ a table at the restaurant.

4 fact: We didn't have any new products and we lost market share.
   but: If we _____ some new products, we _____ market share.

30.3 Complete what you say by writing each sentence as a third conditional.

I went for the interview but I didn't get the job. If they (1) _____ (ask) different questions, perhaps I (2) _____ (be) more successful. And if there (3) _____ (not/be) so many other candidates, I think I (4) _____ (do) better. But in the end it was all a waste of time. I (5) _____ (not/go) if I (6) _____ (know).

30.4 Complete the sentence for each situation using a third conditional. Be careful about whether the result is in the past or the present.

1 fact: We dealt with their complaint very slowly. They are angry.
   but: If we _____ with their complaint so slowly, they _____ angry.

2 fact: We dealt with their complaint very slowly. We lost their business.
   but: If we _____ with their complaint so slowly, we _____ their business.

3 fact: I didn't go on the training course. I don't know how to use the software.
   but: If I _____ on the training course, I _____ how to use the software.

31 Verbs followed by *-ing* or *to* + infinitive 1

A Introduction

● Some verbs are followed by a particular form:

Verb + *-ing* form
We **risk** los**ing** the contract.   this unit

Verb + *to* + infinitive
We **expect to get** the contract.   this unit

Verb + *-ing* or *to* + infinitive: change in meaning
I **stopped smoking/to smoke**.   unit 32

Verb + *-ing* or *to* + infinitive: no change in meaning
When will you **begin producing/to produce** steel at this site?   unit 32

Verb + object + *to* + infinitive
I **persuaded our supplier to extend** our credit limit.   unit 33

B Verb + *-ing*

● The following verbs are usually followed by the *-ing* form:

saying and thinking	*admit, consider, deny, describe, imagine, mention, suggest*
liking and disliking	*dislike, enjoy, (not) mind*
other verbs	*avoid, delay, finish, involve, keep, miss, postpone, risk*
other phrases	*It's not worth …, It's no use …, There's no point (in) …*
	can't help, can't face, can't resist, can't stand
	save/spend time …, save/spend money …

Many consumers will **consider buying** the new TVs when the price comes down.
We **risk losing** everything if we're not careful.
We **spent** half a million dollars **updating** our website.

● Some of the verbs in the list above can also be followed by a noun. These include:
admit, deny, imagine, suggest, dislike, enjoy, keep, mind and *can't …*

I **enjoy** travell**ing** abroad.   and   I **enjoy** foreign **travel**.
I don't mind wait**ing** until she arrives.   and   I don't mind **beer**, but I prefer whisky.

C Verb + *to* + infinitive

● The following verbs are usually followed by *to* + infinitive.

plans and decisions	*aim, arrange, choose, decide, intend, plan, prepare*
expectations	*demand, deserve, expect, hope, want, wish, would like*
promises and refusals	*fail, guarantee, offer, promise, refuse, threaten*
other verbs	*afford, agree, learn, manage, pretend, seem, tend, train, wait*

I **demand to see** the person in charge.
They are **threatening to take** legal action if we **fail to deal with** their complaint.
There are some people **waiting to see** you.

Exercises

31.1 <u>Underline</u> the correct words.

1   There seems *being*/<u>*to be*</u> something wrong – I can't access the network.

2   Have you considered *extending*/*to extend* your warranty by another year?

3   I'd like *having*/*to have* a word with you in my office.

4   We risk *losing*/*to lose* their contract if there are any more problems.

5   I suggest *postponing*/*to postpone* any final decision until we know all the facts.

6   We can't afford *spending*/*to spend* so much money on business lunches.

7   She agreed *preparing*/*to prepare* some figures before the next meeting.

8   I don't mind *waiting*/*to wait* if Ms Neuburger is busy.

9   We decided *advertising*/*to advertise* for staff in the national press.

10 It's not worth *wasting*/*to waste* any more time trying to fix this – it's broken.

31.2 Complete each sentence with the correct form of one of these verbs: *advertise, audit, catch, design, ~~negotiate~~, receive, replace, write.*

1   They wouldn't drop their prices. They completely refused *to negotiate.*

2   I plan _____ the flight that gets to Frankfurt at 3.45.

3   If I delay _____ the report any longer, my boss will be furious.

4   There's no point _____ this brand in 'Stamp Collector' magazine.

5   I expected _____ a letter from them, but nothing has arrived so far.

6   My job involves _____ the accounts of large public companies.

7   We've spent over two months _____ next summer's range of sportswear.

8   We guarantee _____ any faulty parts for a period of two years.

31.3 Complete this email that circulated inside a large retail company. Put the verbs into the correct form, *-ing* or *to* + infinitive.

● ● ●

Subject   RFID technology

We are considering (1) _____ (introduce) radio frequency identification (RFID) tags on all our products in-store. These are small devices that emit radio waves containing information about product size, price, etc. The data is collected by automatic readers at the exit, and the bill is then debited directly from the customer's bank account. I want (2) _____ (prepare) a report for the Board on this technology, and this involves (3) _____ (get) feedback from you on how you think shoppers will respond. There is a benefit for them as they save time (4) _____ (stand) in line at the checkout – they just walk out the store and don't have to wait (5) _____ (pay). But will they mind (6) _____ (give) us automatic access to their bank accounts? We can't avoid (7) _____ (deal) with privacy issues like this.

Please let me know what you think – I hope (8) _____ (have) your comments by the end of the month.

A Verb + *-ing* or *to* + infinitive: change in meaning

● Some verbs can be followed by *-ing* or *to* + infinitive and the meaning changes.

remember	*I **remember visiting** Florence on my honeymoon.* (action first, then remember it later) *Before you go, **remember to turn off** the lights.* (remember first, then do the action)
stop	*We **stopped using** that firm of accountants.* (quit; not do it any more) *We **stopped** at the pub **to have** some lunch.* (pause in the middle of doing something else)
regret	*I **regret saying** 'no' to that job in Paris.* (be sorry about something in the past) *I **regret to tell** you that the items you need are out of stock.* (be sorry about what you are going to say)
try	*I'll **try talking** to her – maybe she'll change her mind.* (do something to see what will happen) *I'll **try to talk** to her today, but I know she's very busy.* (make an effort, but perhaps without success)

B Verb + *-ing* or *to* + infinitive: no change in meaning

● Some verbs can be followed by *-ing* or *to* + infinitive and there is no change in meaning. These include: *begin, continue, intend, like, love, prefer, start.*

*The unemployment rate **continued falling/to fall** last month.*

● Note that *like* means 'enjoy' and can be followed by either form. But *would like* means 'want' and is followed only by *to* + infinitive.

*I **like going/to go** to Italian restaurants.*   (I enjoy this in general)
*I'**d like to go** to an Italian restaurant this evening.* (I want to do this)

● Note that we do not usually have two *-ing* forms together.

*The unemployment rate is **continuing to fall**.* (NOT ~~continuing falling~~)

C Phrases with *to* + *-ing* (because *to* is a preposition)

● The word *to* can be part of an infinitive (*I'd like **to go** there.*). However, in the following phrases *to* is a preposition, and prepositions are followed by the *-ing* form: *look forward to, object to, be/get used to, in addition to, a reaction to.*

*I look forward **to meeting** you in Toulouse.*   (NOT ~~to meet~~)
*I'm not used **to travelling** on the Paris Metro.*   (NOT ~~to travel~~)
*In addition **to buying** shares in Cisco, I also bought shares in IBM.* (NOT ~~to buy~~)

Exercises

32.1 Match the phrases in *italics* on the left with their meaning a) or b) on the right.

1 We *stopped to look* at the view. ☐
2 We *stopped producing* cars at this site last year. ☐

    a) not do it any more
    b) pause in the middle of doing something else

---

3 I've got a bit of a headache – I think I'll *try taking* an aspirin. ☐
4 The situation is complicated, but I'll *try to explain*. ☐

    a) do something to see what will happen
    b) make an effort, but perhaps without success

---

5 I must *remember to call* Antonia. ☐
6 Douglas Petersen? Oh yes, I *remember meeting* him in San Diego. ☐

    a) action first, then remember it later
    b) remember first, then do the action

32.2 Put a tick (✓) by correct forms. Put a cross (✗) by incorrect forms.

1 What do you intend doing about it?
2 What do you intend to do about it?
3 I like going abroad for my holidays.
4 I'd like going abroad for my next holiday.
5 I lived in the UK for a while, but I never got used to drive on the left.
6 In addition to increasing our profits last year, market share was up by 3%.

32.3 Put the verbs into the correct form, *-ing* or *to* + infinitive.

1 I tried _____*to open*_____ (open) the window, but it was too high to reach.
2 I tried _____*opening*_____ (open) the window, but it was still too hot in the room.
3 Lydia was at the conference. I remember _____ (see) her there.
4 Did you remember _____ (give) Majeed the message?
5 I stopped in Prague for a day _____ (meet) all our Czech colleagues.
6 We stopped _____ (meet) so often. It was a waste of time.
7 If I'm not at the office, try _____ (call) me at home.
8 I tried _____ (get) a job at Accenture, but I didn't have the right background.

32.4 Put the verbs into the correct form: *-ing*, or *to* + infinitive, or *to* + *-ing*.

Oil: a high price to pay

Do you remember the price of oil (1) _____ (be) $10 a barrel? Amazingly, that was the situation as recently as 1998. We'd all like (2) _____ (go) back to those days, but we never will. Oil companies are trying (3) _____ (find) new oil fields, and have had some success in the Caspian Sea and West Africa. But production has probably peaked, and demand is definitely increasing. You'll just have to get used (4) _____ (pay) more for your petrol. Otherwise, there's no problem: just stop (5) _____ (use) your car!

A Transitive and intransitive verbs

● Transitive verbs are followed by an object. They are usually shown in the dictionary with a *T*. The object can have a variety of forms.

*We manufacture **agricultural machinery**.*   (object = adjective + noun)
*We offer **solutions to all your financial needs**.*   (object = a noun phrase)
*I can't afford **it**.*   (object = a pronoun)

Note that a transitive verb is not complete without an object.

● Intransitive verbs do not take an object, although they can be followed by an adverb. They are usually shown in the dictionary with an *I*.

Verb on its own   *Profits fell.*
Verb + adverb   *Profits fell slightly/in Europe/last quarter.* (how/where/when)

(But NOT verb + object: ~~Our company fell its profits~~.)

● Intransitive verbs include: *appear, arrive, come, depart, disappear, exist, fall, go, happen, live, occur, rain, remain, rise, sleep, speak, wait, walk, work.*

● Many verbs can have both a transitive and an intransitive form.

We began the meeting.   and   *The meeting began.*

B Verbs with two objects

● Some verbs have both a direct object (DO) and an indirect object (IO). If the indirect object comes first, it is used without *to*.

*He lent **me** (IO) **his umbrella** (DO).*   (NOT ~~He lent to me~~)
*She sends **you** (IO) **her best regards** (DO).*   (NOT ~~She sends to you~~)

● Verbs like this include: *bring, buy, cause, cost, email, give, lend, make, offer, owe, pass, pay, promise, read, sell, send, show, tell, write.*

C Verb + object + *to* + infinitive

● Some verbs can be followed by object + *to* + infinitive. These include: *advise, allow, ask, enable, encourage, expect, force, help, invite, order, persuade, remind, teach, tell, train, want, warn.*

*I **told him to confirm** the order in writing.* (NOT ~~I told to him to confirm~~)
*We have **persuaded the American investors to put** money into the company.*

● Some of the verbs in the list above are commonly used with *not to do*.

*He **warned me not to say** anything until the plans are finalized.*

D *Make/let* + object + infinitive (without *to*)

● After *make* and *let* we use the infinitive without *to*.

*I **made them send** me a replacement part.*   (NOT ~~I made them to send~~)
*They **let us have** an extra discount.*   (NOT ~~They let us to have~~)

Exercises

33.1 Tick (✓) the sentences that are correct. Cross (✗) the ones that are incorrect.

1 She's getting. ✗
2 She's waiting. ✓
3 It will happen.
4 It will have.
5 I've been working.
6 I've been enjoying.
7 The package contained.
8 The package came.
9 I slept.
10 I contacted.
11 It's raining.
12 It's making.
13 We cut the marketing budget by 10%.
14 We fell the marketing budget by 10%.
15 In the meeting we spoke all the issues.
16 In the meeting we discussed all the issues.
17 She came my office yesterday.
18 She visited my office yesterday.
19 The bus leaves the hotel at eight.
20 The bus arrives the hotel at eight.

33.2 Only two of these six sentences are correct. Tick (✓) the correct sentences.

1 He gave his promise me.
2 He gave me his promise.
3 He gave to me his promise.
4 We paid to the consultants a lot of money.
5 We paid a lot of money the consultants.
6 We paid the consultants a lot of money.

33.3 The words in each sentence are in the wrong order. Rewrite them in the correct order.

1 She helped to install me the software. _____
2 They have invited to me speak at the conference. _____
3 He warned to me not park there. _____
4 Could you to remind me call Head Office later? _____
5 They trained to us maintain the new machines. _____
6 She encouraged to apply me for the job. _____

33.4 In the article below, the word *to* is missing in five places. Put back the word *to* in the right places.

Sales techniques: we use them every day

What do you think when you hear the phrase 'sales techniques'? Some people have a very bad impression of sales, and it's true that a clever sales consultant can sell you almost anything. But like it or not, we all use sales techniques. Have you ever persuaded anyone go on vacation where you wanted, not where they wanted? Have you ever 'sold' an idea or opinion by encouraging the other person see your point of view? In fact 'sales' is a very misunderstood concept. It's not about making people buy things they don't need, it's about giving them information and then letting them choose. If a sales person wants you decide too quickly, just tell them wait. No-one can force you buy something that you really don't want.

34 The *-ing* form

*Good **marketing** is **having a story**, and **branding** is the **telling** of that story.*

Business 2.0 website

A *-ing* form as a noun

- The *-ing* form can be used as a noun. In this case it is also called a gerund.

  Marketing *includes more than just **advertising**.*

- The *-ing* form can be part of a whole phrase.

  Marketing on the Internet *is more than just using clever graphics.*

B *-ing* form as an adjective

- The *-ing* form can be used like an adjective, before a noun.

  *We are a small **manufacturing company** based outside Istanbul.*
  *The stock market went down yesterday – there was a lot of **selling pressure**.*

- A small group of adjectives have both an *-ing* form and an *-ed* form. Examples include: *interesting/interested, boring/bored, surprising/surprised, tiring/tired.*

  *The presentation was very **interesting**. I was **interested** in the part about motivation.*
  *The information she gave me was **surprising**. I was really **surprised** by it.*
  *The flight was ten hours – quite **tiring**. I need an early night because I'm so **tired**.*

  Study the examples above. The *-ing* form describes what we are reacting to (outside us). The *-ed* form describes our feelings (inside us).

C *-ing* form after a preposition

*Research shows that consumers delete most marketing e-mail **without** even **opening** it.*

Marketing Week website

- We use the *-ing* form after prepositions.

  *Nissan are interested **in forming** a joint venture with Mitsubishi Motors.*
  *Federal Express became successful **by focusing** on overnight delivery.*
  After making *staff and business cutbacks, Anne Mulcahy saved Xerox.*

- Be careful with the word *to*. It is usually part of the infinitive (*I decided **to go** home*). But sometimes it is a preposition followed by an *-ing* form.

  *I look forward **to seeing** you in Paris.* (NOT ~~to see~~)
  *I'm not used **to getting** up so early.* (NOT ~~to get up~~)

  To know whether *to* is an infinitive or a preposition, try putting a noun after it.

  *I decided **to ~~our meeting~~**.* (not possible, so *to* is part of an infinitive)
  *I look forward **to** our meeting.* (possible, so *to* is a preposition)

D *-ing* form that begins a clause

- A clause beginning with an *-ing* form can give information about a noun. This is a short form of a relative clause. (See unit 37.)

  *The woman **talking to Anton** works for Citigroup.*   (= who is talking)
  *Companies **doing business in China** need local partners.*   (= which are doing)
  *The amount of money **going into nanotechnology** is enormous.*   (= which is going)

Exercises

34.1 Match the word *working* in each sentence with uses a)–f).

1 *Working* with you has been a pleasure. ☐
2 I'm tired of *working* so hard. ☐
3 The people *working* here are all nice. ☐
4 I'm *working* on an unusual project. ☐
5 I enjoy *working* from home. ☐
6 'Blue collar' means *working* class. ☐

a) present continuous (unit 2)
b) -*ing* follows previous verb (unit 31)
c) a noun (gerund)
d) an adjective
e) after a preposition
f) short form of a relative clause (unit 37)

34.2 Complete the sentences with -*ing* adjectives formed from these verbs: *charm, increase, meet, sell, shop*.

1 They're building a new ____*shopping*____ mall by the motorway exit.
2 Its modern design is one of its strongest _____ points.
3 I was introduced to Monsieur Corbet and his _____ wife.
4 Because of the recession there is _____ pressure to cut some jobs.
5 Excuse me, can you show me the way to the _____ room?

34.3 Underline the correct word.

1 Look at these sales figures; they're really *surprised/surprising*.
2 A: 'Have you seen the sales figures?'   B: 'Yes, I'm really *surprised/surprising*.'
3 I was absolutely *fascinated/fascinating* by your talk.
4 I found your talk absolutely *fascinated/fascinating*.
5 I look forward to *hear/hearing* from you soon.
6 I hope we're going to *hear/hearing* from them soon.
7 In my last job we sometimes used to *work/working* on Saturday morning.
8 I can't help you – I'm not used to *work/working* with this software.

34.4 After each preposition put one of these verbs in the -*ing* form: *continue, finish, pay, produce, rely, retire*.

Retirement   start planning now

Are you looking forward to (1) _____*retiring*_____ ? What will you receive from the state after (2) _____ your working life? A large pension? Think again. Instead of (3) _____ on the state to support you, you will have to save money yourself, by (4) _____ into a private pension plan over many years. The problem is global aging. People are reaching retirement age without (5) _____ the same number of children as they did in the past. So there are not enough young workers to pay tax to support the older generation. Is there a solution? Yes, if you are interested in (6) _____ to work until you are 70.

35 Reported speech 1

A Introduction

- Look at this example. The public relations officer of Biogen is speaking to a journalist. During the conversation she says, *'Our next arthritis drug **will** be very successful.'*

  There are three ways that this conversation can be reported:

  a) *A source inside Biogen **said**, 'Our next arthritis drug **will** be very successful.'*
  (in writing, repeating the exact words and using quotation marks)

  b) *The Biogen PR officer **says** that their next arthritis drug **will** be very successful.*
  (in speech, using *say* in the present, and keeping the original form *will*)

  c) *The Biogen PR officer **said** that their next arthritis drug **would** be very successful.*
  (in speech, using *said* in the past, and changing *will* to *would*)

- Sentence c) above, where the verb changes, is called 'reported speech' (or sometimes 'indirect speech').

- In this unit the reporting verb is always *say*. Other reporting verbs like *announce, suggest, promise,* etc are covered in unit 36.

B Tense changes

- When the form of the verb changes (like *will → would*), it 'moves back' in time.

Actual words	Reported (indirect) speech
*'I **work** for BP.'*	*He said (that) he **worked** for BP.*
*'I **am working** for BP.'*	*He said (that) he **was working** for BP.*
*'I **have worked** for BP.'*	*He said (that) he **had worked** for BP.*
*'I **worked** for BP.'*	*He said (that) he **worked/had worked** for BP.*
*'I **will/can work** for BP.'*	*He said (that) he **would/could work** for BP.*

- Note that if the actual verb was in the past simple (*worked*), the report can stay the same (*worked*) or change (*had worked*).

- There is no change for *must, should, might, could, would*.

"I know we said we'd get you a laptop...
But this will have to do until business is better."

C Other changes

- It is sometimes necessary to make other changes. In section A sentences b) and c) note how the original words ***our*** arthritis drug change to ***their*** arthritis drug.

- Here is another example showing tense changes and other changes.

  Petra speaking to Richard on the phone:

  *'It's a pity that Dana isn't in the office **today** – I really **need** to speak to **her** urgently. Can you give her a message? Say that I called, and that I'll email **her** with the budget proposals. Thanks a lot – bye.'*

  Richard reports the conversation to Dana the next day:

  *'Oh, by the way, Petra called **yesterday**. She said that **she needed** to speak to **you** urgently, and that she'**d** email **you** with the budget proposals.'*

Exercises

35.1 Below are some actual words spoken in a meeting.

'I've just seen the report for the first time this morning, and I don't agree with the conclusions. I can see that we're spending far too much money on this project.'

A few days later you tell a colleague about the discussion. <u>Underline</u> the correct words in the speech bubble.

He said he (1) *has seen/had seen* the report for the first time (2) *this morning/that morning*, and he (3) *didn't agree/hasn't agreed* with the conclusions. He said he (4) *can see/could see* that we (5) *were spending/are spending* far too much money on the project.

35.2 Write the actual words that each person says. Use contractions where possible.

1 Celine said she had contacted the maintenance company.
  She said, '____*I've contacted*____ the maintenance company.'

2 George said he would be back in the office around eleven.
  He said, '_____ back in the office around eleven.'

3 Helen said she was going to process the order today.
  She said, '_____ the order today.'

4 Paul said that he wanted to check the figures again.
  He said, '_____ the figures again.'

35.3 Look at the actual words spoken. <u>Underline</u> the correct words in the reported version.

1 Florencia said, 'I'm meeting Mr Smith tomorrow.'
  Florencia said she *is/was* meeting Mr Smith *tomorrow/<u>the next day</u>*.

2 Mai said to me, 'I'll email you about the sales conference.'
  Mai said she *will/would* email *me/her* about the sales conference.

3 The sales manager said, 'We received your order yesterday.'
  He said *we/they* received *our/your* order the day *after/before*.

4 Yumiko said, 'Here in Japan this area of technology is very advanced.'
  She said that *here/there* in Japan *this/that* area of technology *is/was* very advanced.

35.4 Rewrite the sentences in reported speech. Use contractions where possible.

1 She said, 'I'm going to be late and I'm not sure when I'll arrive.'
  She said she was going to be late and _____

2 He said, 'I'm finishing some paperwork and I won't be long.'
  He said he _____

3 She said, 'I don't think it can be repaired, but I'll do my best.'
  She said _____

36 Reported speech 2

A Say or tell?

● We *say* something. We *say to* somebody. We *tell* somebody.

Colin **said/said to me** *(that) the project was going well.* (NOT said me)
Colin **told me** *(that) the project was going well.* (NOT told to me)

B Other reporting verbs

● Apart from *say* and *tell* there are many other verbs to report what people say. The verbs can be followed by various forms.

Verb + *-ing*	*admit, apologize for, deny, mention, propose, suggest*
Verb + *to* + infinitive	*agree, ask, demand, decide, offer, promise, refuse*
Verb + object + *to* + infinitive	*advise, ask, encourage, order, persuade, remind, tell, warn*
Verb + object + *that …*	*inform, persuade, promise, remind, tell*

*I **suggested changing** our local agent.*
*He **promised to call** me tomorrow.*
*She **encouraged me to apply** for the job.*
*They **persuaded us that** we should expand our product range.*

● Note in the lists above that some verbs can be followed by more than one form.

*The auditor **asked to see** (**asked me to show him**) our balance sheet.*
*I **reminded them to pay** (**reminded them that they should pay**) the invoice.*

● With all reporting verbs we make tense changes and other changes as in unit 35.

*'I **will** be **there tomorrow'** → He promised me that he **would** be **here today**.*

● The verbs in the list above refer to speaking. We can also report what people think with verbs like: *know, notice, think, realize.*

(I think): *Isabel **won't** check the stock levels.*
(I say later): *I **thought** Isabel **wouldn't** check the stock levels.*

C Reporting a question

● When we report a question we use the same tense changes as in unit 35.

*'What **is** your job title?' → She asked me what my job title **was**.*
*'When **will** the artwork arrive?' → He asked me when the artwork **would** arrive.*

● Note the word order in the reported question.

(NOT what was my job title)
(NOT when would arrive the artwork)

● When we report a *yes/no* question we use *if* or *whether* and the same tense changes.

*'**Are** you **having** a Christmas sale?' → She asked me **if** we **were having** a sale.*
*'**Do** you **know** Werner from Zurich?' → He asked me **whether** I **knew** Werner.*

Exercises

36.1 Underline the correct form.

1 Sally *said*/told that she had prepared the customer questionnaire.

2 Sebastian *said me/told me* that the trip to Brussels had been very useful.

3 Kate *said us/said* that the legal documents were all in order.

4 She *said to Maria/told to Maria* that she was going to go home early today.

36.2 Rewrite the sentences in reported speech using the verbs in brackets.

1 'I think you should take more exercise.' (advise)

The doctor ___*advised me to take more exercise.*___

2 'I'm sorry I missed the presentation.' (apologize for)

Manuela _____

3 'We will not renegotiate the contract.' (refuse)

They _____

4 'Don't forget to back up all the files.' (remind)

The tech support guy _____

5 'Why not extend the Christmas sale by a week?' (suggest)

The store manager _____

6 'I'll definitely be at the meeting on Friday.' (promise)

He _____

7 'Robert, you're fired.' (tell)

She _____

36.3 These *yes/no* questions are taken from a job interview. Rewrite them in reported speech.

1 'Do you speak French?' → They asked me _____*if I spoke French.*_____

2 'Are you prepared to relocate to France?' → They asked me _____

3 'Can you use Microsoft Office?' → They asked me _____

4 'Are you hoping for a salary increase?' → They asked me _____

36.4 EuroCom is involved in a financial scandal and the CEO has to answer some questions at a press conference. Look at the questions and then report them in the correct way.

'What is the real problem at EuroCom?'   1 They asked him ___*what the real problem at EuroCom was.*___

'What have the auditors discovered?'   2 They asked him _____

'When can we see the auditors' report?'   3 They asked him _____

'How much money will investors lose?'   4 They asked him _____

'What are you going to do next?'   5 They asked him _____

37 Relative clauses 1

A Introduction

● A relative clause is a short phrase beginning with words like *who, that, which* that identifies or describes people and things. There are two types: defining and non-defining relative clauses.

Defining relative clauses

*The people **that designed the TCP/IP Internet protocols** were Vinton Cerf and Robert Kahn.*

The clause in **bold** identifies/defines the people we are talking about. The information is necessary for the sentence to make sense.

Non-defining relative clauses

*Vinton Cerf, **who was one of the designers of the TCP/IP Internet protocols**, is a senior Vice President at MCI.*

The clause in **bold** gives extra information about Vinton Cerf, but the sentence makes sense without it.

● This unit explains defining clauses. Unit 38 explains non-defining clauses.

B Relative pronouns

● The words *who, which, that* and *whose* can begin a relative clause. They are called relative pronouns.

● To refer to people, we use *who* or *that*.
*The candidate **who/that David is interviewing this afternoon** has an MBA in finance.*
To refer to things, we use *that* or *which*.
*The markets **that/which we need to focus on** are Brazil and Russia.*
In speech, *who* is more common for people and *that* is more common for things.

● The relative pronoun *whose* shows possession.
*The BBC is a news organization **whose reputation is excellent**.*
*The online retailer **whose website I use most often** is Amazon.*

C Combining sentences

● Look at these examples of how we can combine two short sentences using a relative clause.

I'd like you to meet a colleague. She works in the Moscow office.
→ *I'd like you to meet a colleague **who** works in the Moscow office.*

We've introduced a new product. It is aimed at the youth market.
→ *We've introduced a new product **that** is aimed at the youth market.*

● When we combine sentences the relative pronoun replaces the personal pronoun.
(NOT I'd like you to meet a colleague who ~~she~~ works in the Moscow office.)
(NOT We've introduced a new product that ~~it~~ is aimed at the youth market.)

Exercises

37.1 Ann is talking to a friend. Complete what she says using these words: *who, which, that, whose.*
Two spaces mean that two words are possible.

> Did I tell you that they moved me into a new office? The person (1) _____ office I share now is very friendly. I brought some things from the old office to make me feel at home. The photograph (2) _____ / _____ my husband gave me is on the wall. But the room sometimes gets dirty. I think the cleaners (3) _____ / _____ do our section forget about it.

37.2 Complete the sentences in this article with *who, which* or *whose.*

Manager? Or entrepreneur?

How is an entrepreneur different to a manager? An entrepreneur is someone (1) _____ starts their own business, often with their own money. It's very risky, and something (2) _____ most people wouldn't do. A manager, on the other hand, prefers to work for a large company (3) _____ position in the market is already well established. An entrepreneur doesn't feel comfortable in a large company: those meetings (4) _____ last all morning, the boss (5) _____ tells them what to do and the team (6) _____ members are always arguing about nothing. Basically, a manager wants security, but an entrepreneur wants control.

37.3 If the sentence is correct, put a tick (✓). If the sentence has a word which should not be there, cross it out.

1 I'm taking a flight that leaves at 3.45.
2 I'm taking a flight that it leaves at 3.45.
3 They've appointed a new Board member who she has a background in banking.
4 My boss is a person who takes decisions very quickly.
5 Gold is a commodity whose its price is linked closely to the dollar.

37.4 Combine the sentences using the relative pronoun in brackets.

1 We're developing a new financial product. It is aimed at wealthy clients. (that)
   → We're developing _a new financial product that is aimed at wealthy clients._
2 Suki's got a new job. It's very stressful. (that)
   → Suki's got _____
3 We found a translator. She can speak Lithuanian and Polish. (who)
   → We found _____
4 The company gave me a cell phone. It can connect directly to our network. (that)
   → The company gave me _____
5 Tomorrow I'm meeting a new client. He could give us a lot of business. (who)
   → Tomorrow I'm meeting _____

38 Relative clauses 2

A Prepositions in relative clauses

- Normally we put prepositions like *to, from, about* at the end of the relative clause. Note that this may be in the middle or at the end of the sentence.

  *The main thing **(that) we talked about** was the budget forecast.*
  *The budget forecast was the main thing **(that) we talked about**.*

B When/why/where

- We can use *when, why* and *where* in a relative clause with their normal meanings.

  *I'll always remember the day **(when) they made me team leader**.*
  *I don't understand the reason **(why) he resigned from his job**.*
  *I can recommend the hotel in Vienna **where I stayed**.*

- Note from the examples above that we can leave out *when* and *why*, but we normally keep *where*.

- However, we must leave out *where* if there is a preposition at the end of the clause.

  *I can recommend the hotel **I stayed in**.* (NOT ~~where I stayed in~~)

C What

- We can use *what* to replace 'the thing(s) that'.

  *The pharmacy didn't have **what** I needed.* (= the thing that I needed)
  *It was difficult to follow **what** she said.* (= the things that she said)

D Non-defining relative clauses

- Some relative clauses identify which person or thing we mean. Some relative clauses simply add extra information. Compare:

  *a) The sales assistant **who I spoke to yesterday** said I could have a discount.*
  *b) The sales assistant, **who was only about 18**, said I could have a discount.*

- Example a) is a defining relative clause. The information identifies which sales assistant I mean. The information is necessary for the conversation.

  Example b) is a non-defining relative clause. The information is not necessary. I am not identifying which sales assistant I mean.

- In a non-defining clause we use commas in writing or a pause in speech.

  *Jack Welch, **who was born in 1935**, increased the value of General Electric from $13 billion to several hundred billion during his twenty years at the top.*

- A non-defining clause can come at the end of a sentence.

  *General Electric was run by Jack Welch, **who was born in 1935**.*

- In a non-defining clause we must use a relative pronoun, but we never use *that*.

  *Nissan, **which uses many Renault components**, is having a good year.* (NOT ~~that uses~~)

Exercises

38.1 Add one of these prepositions, in the correct place, to each sentence: *at, for, from, in, to, ~~with~~*.

1 The people I went to the conference/are sitting over there. *with*

2 Here's the address of the reseller I bought my printer.

3 The products we are interested are at the lower end of your price range.

4 This is the department I am responsible.

5 Here's the website I was looking earlier.

6 The person you need to talk is the Sales Manager, Mrs. Wildstrom.

38.2 Add the word *where* or *what* to each sentence, in the correct place.

1 I recently went back to visit the company/I had my first job. *where*

2 This software package can do exactly you want.

3 After lunch I'll show you the laboratory we do all our quality control.

4 I was very interested in she was saying in her talk.

5 The Alentejo is the region most of our cork is produced.

6 We can ship you need by FedEx Priority Service.

38.3 Use the information in 1–4 below to add four non-defining relative clauses to the article. Remember to use *who* or *which*.

AMD: a competitor to Intel

, which has taken second place to Intel for many years,

Advanced Micro Devices (AMD)/wants to become a major competitor in the

microprocessor business. Its Chief Executive, Hector de Jesus Ruiz hopes to use

AMD's success in the server market to convince customers to buy PCs and notebooks

containing AMD semiconductors. But both AMD and Intel will find it difficult to make

money in the PC market. They need to target new areas such as digital TVs, set-top

boxes and cell phones. But in the end, the battle between AMD and Intel will depend

on marketing as much as technology. Intel have recently appointed Eric Kim to make

its brand more exciting and broaden its marketing message.

1 Eric Kim used to be Samsung's top marketing exec.

2 ~~AMD has taken second place to Intel for many years.~~

3 The PC market has been growing very slowly in recent years.

4 Hector de Jesus Ruiz is a Mexican immigrant with a PhD in electronics.

A Countable nouns

- Countable nouns include objects, people and units of measurement.

  one bank, three banks   *one manager, two managers*   *one metre, eight metres*

- Countable nouns and their verbs can be singular or plural.

  *One manager **is** in charge of the department.*
  *Two managers **are** in charge of the department.*

- In speech we usually say *a/an* when there is one of something.

  *I have to write **a report** this afternoon.*   (NOT ~~one report~~)
  *I got **an email** from him yesterday.*   (*an* before a vowel sound *a, e, i, o, u*)

  But we can use the word *one* when the exact number is important.

  *I only got **one email** from him, several weeks ago. He hasn't been in touch since then.*

B Uncountable nouns

- Uncountable nouns include materials and substances, abstract ideas, activities and feelings. 'Uncountable' means we cannot use numbers.

  water   (NOT ~~one water, two waters~~)
  progress   (NOT ~~one progress, two progresses~~)

- Uncountable nouns only have one form (no *-s* plural) and take a singular verb.

  *Progress on the project **is** quite slow.* (NOT ~~are quite slow~~)

- Typical uncountable nouns are:

materials and substances	*air, coffee, cotton, oil, paper, plastic, rice, steel, water*
abstract ideas	*freedom, fun, health, life, progress, safety, space, time*
activities	*engineering, football, help, research, sleep, travel, work*
feelings	*anger, courage, happiness, honesty, hope, respect*

- Be careful! The nouns in the list below are uncountable in English but countable in many other languages.

  accommodation, advertising, advice, baggage, behaviour, business, cash, equipment, furniture, hair, hardware, health, information, insurance, knowledge, luggage, machinery, money, permission, progress, research, software, traffic, travel, trouble, weather, work

C Determiners (*a/some/many/much*, etc)

- We use different determiners for countable and uncountable nouns.

Countable	Uncountable
*I need **a** dictionary.*	*I need **some** time.*
*We don't have **many** employees.*	*We don't do **much** research.*
*Give the waiter **a few** euros as a tip.*	*Give the waiter **a little** space for the vegetables.*

- So ~~an information~~ and ~~some informations~~ are wrong and *some information* is right.

Exercises

39.1 Each pair of words contains one countable and one uncountable noun. Write *a/an* or *some* before each word.

1	__*a*__ bag	__*some*__ luggage	
2	_____ accommodation	_____ hotel	
3	_____ furniture	_____ office chair	
4	_____ job	_____ work	
5	_____ machine	_____ machinery	
6	_____ trouble	_____ problem	
7	_____ wine	_____ litre	
8	_____ email	_____ correspondence	
9	_____ money	_____ dollar	
10	_____ information	_____ fact	
11	_____ suggestion	_____ advice	
12	_____ week	_____ time	

"We have lots of information technology. We just don't have any information."

39.2 Complete each sentence with *is* or *are*.

1 Here _____ the report on inventory levels in the warehouse.

2 Here _____ the figures for inventory levels in the warehouse.

3 Here _____ the information about inventory levels in the warehouse.

4 A lot of our computers _____ already out-of-date.

5 A lot of our hardware _____ already out-of-date.

6 They unloaded the plane quickly – our luggage _____ already on the belt.

7 They unloaded the plane quickly – our bags _____ already on the belt.

44

39.3 <u>Underline</u> the correct words.

Nanotechnology
small scale, big potential

Nanotechnology is the branch of engineering that deals with individual molecules. There has been (1) *many/much* progress over recent years in the (2) *many/much* laboratories involved in this research. In the US, a lot of government money (3) *are/is* available through the National Nanotechnology Initiative, and millions of dollars (4) *are/is* also being spent in the private sector. The University of Rochester is a leader in the field: they are doing (5) *an/some* interesting research where they are trying to treat diseased cells at the genetic level. Of course, there are (6) *a little/a few* problems in this area of science and it will take (7) *a little/a few* time before all the difficulties are overcome. In particular, (8) *much/many* people (9) *is/are* worried by safety issues, and it is crucial that governments provide (10) *a/some* detailed advice in this area.

Countable and uncountable nouns 2

A Specific and general meanings

- Many nouns can have a specific meaning (where they are countable) and a general meaning (where they are uncountable).

Specific/countable	**General/uncountable**
The machine is making **a strange noise**.	We are reducing **noise** in the factory.
There aren't **many spaces** in the car park.	There isn't **much space** in my office.
I bought **a football** for my son's birthday.	**Football** is very popular in Italy.
I've worked in **many different businesses**.	**Business** is going well at the moment.

- Here are some more examples.

  a coffee/coffee (a cup of coffee/the substance)
  a fish/fish (one specific animal/a type of food)
  a glass/glass (a container for a drink/the material)
  a paper/paper (a newspaper or conference report/the material)
  a wood/wood (a small forest/the material)
  a work/work (a work of art/activity involving effort)

- Note in the examples above that in the general meaning we do not use the word *a*.

B Singular or plural verb? (*machine/machinery/company*)

- Countable nouns (like *machine*) can have a singular noun and verb, or a plural noun and verb.

  The new **machine is** much faster./The new **machines are** much faster.

  Uncountable nouns (like *machinery*) always have a singular verb.

  The new **machinery is** much faster. (NOT ~~are~~)

- Some nouns have a singular form (without -s), but they consist of more than one person/thing. Examples include: *army, audience, board, company, data, crowd, family, government, group, management, media, press, public, staff, team, union*.

  These can be followed by either a singular or a plural verb.

  The company **is/are** doing well at the moment.

C How to count an uncountable noun

- Uncountable nouns cannot be counted directly. However, we can count them using phrases like: *a piece of, a glass of, a bottle of, a kilo of, a barrel of*.

  She gave me **two pieces of** information. (NOT ~~two informations~~)

  The US consumes about **eighteen million barrels of** oil each day. (NOT ~~eighteen million oils~~)

- For many uncountable nouns there is a countable noun with a related meaning.

The advertising campaign cost a lot of **money**.	(money is uncountable)
The advertising campaign cost **half a million euros**.	(euro is countable)
I've done a lot of **work** since leaving university.	(work is uncountable)
I've had **three jobs** since leaving university.	(job is countable)

Exercises

40.1 <u>Underline</u> the correct words.

   1 I'm going to leave my job and start <u>*a business*</u>/*business* designing websites.

   2 *A business/Business* has improved since we moved to a more central location.

   3 Thanks for your help. I'll leave now; I know you have *a work/work* to do.

   4 I bought her a poster from the art gallery – *a work/work* by Picasso.

   5 *A life/Life* can be very complicated sometimes.

   6 He had *a life/life* that was long and happy.

   7 In this job, *an experience/experience* is more important than qualifications.

   8 Visiting the Taj Mahal was *an experience/experience* that I'll never forget.

   9 Do you want to try some of this wine? I'll ask the waiter for *a glass/glass*.

  10 Bottles and jars made from *a glass/glass* are better for recycling.

40.2 In each space write either *is,* or *are,* or *is/are* (if both are possible).

   1 Senior managers __*are*__ doing everything possible to improve profits.

   2 The management __*is/are*__ doing everything possible to improve profits.

   3 Our Production Director _____ very concerned about lay-offs at the factory.

   4 The union _____ very concerned about lay-offs at the factory.

   5 The team _____ working very well together.

   6 The team members _____ working very well together.

40.3 Complete each sentence 1–6 with the correct ending a)–f).

1	2 slices of	☐	a) oil lie under the sea, but it's difficult to extract.
2	1 trillion barrels of	☐	b) tequila, the Mexican drink, have a worm inside.
3	Many sheets of	☐	c) pie is not a good idea if you're on a diet.
4	18 million kilos of	☐	d) paper can be saved by making double-sided photocopies.
5	Most bottles of	☐	e) water a day are necessary for a person's well-being.
6	2 litres of	☐	f) fish are farmed in Finland every year, mainly trout.

45

40.4 Complete the text with these words: *fish, a fish, glass, ~~a glass~~, iron, an iron, paper, a paper, wood, a wood.*

Is a glass made of glass? Is an iron made of iron?

In the morning you put some orange juice in (1) __*a glass*__ made of (2) _____ and read (3) _____ made of (4) _____ . The paper, in turn, is made from (5) _____ that comes from (6) _____ (or a forest). But these days (7) _____ for pressing your clothes is not actually made of (8) _____ . And when a friend asks you in a restaurant: 'Do you like (9) _____ ?', remember that they aren't asking about (10) _____ you know personally, like your pet goldfish.

41 Determiners 1

A Introduction

● A determiner is a word that is used in front of a noun to show which thing you are talking about. In this book determiners are covered in several units:

some, any, many, much, a few, a little	this unit
all, no, each, every, both, either, neither	unit 42
a/an, the (articles)	unit 43 and 44
my/your (possessive adjectives)	unit 45

B *Some/any*

● *Some* is common in affirmative sentences. *Any* is common in questions and negative sentences.

A: 'Do you have **any** brochures in your office for our Japanese visitors?' (question)
B: 'Yes, and I have **some** product samples as well.' (affirmative)
A: 'Good, because I don't have **any** material like that in my office.' (negative)

● We can use *some* in a question if it is an offer or request.

Offer: *Would you like to see **some** samples of our products?*
Request: *Could I see **some** samples of your products?*

● We can also use *some* in a question if we expect the answer to be *yes*. Compare:

*Have you got **some letters** for me?* (I expect that you have)
*Have you got **any letters** for me?* (I have no expectation about the answer)

C *Any* meaning 'no limit'

● We use *any* in an affirmative sentence if the meaning is 'no limit'. Compare:

*I'm free **some days** next week – Tuesday, Thursday and Friday.*
*I'm free **any day** next week – we can meet whenever you want.*

D *Many/much, a few/a little*

● *Many* is used for countable nouns and *much* is used for uncountable nouns. (See unit 39.) They are most common in a question or negative sentence.

| countable | *How **many** bags do you have?* | *I don't have **many bags**.* |
| uncountable | *How **much** luggage do you have?* | *I don't have much **luggage**.* |

● In an affirmative sentence we often say *a lot of* or *lots of*.

*I have **a lot of bags/a lot of luggage** with me on this trip.*

● *A few* is used for countable nouns and *a little* is used for uncountable nouns.

| countable | *We only have **a few days**, so we'll have to be quick.* |
| uncountable | *We only have **a little time**, so we'll have to be quick.* |

Exercises

41.1 Tick (✓) sentences where *some/any* are used correctly. Change incorrect sentences.

1 We only offer 60 days credit to ~~any~~ customers. *some*

2 Did you get any difficult questions at the end of your presentation? ✓

3 Excuse me, waiter, could you bring some water, please?

4 Excuse me, waiter, is there some swordfish on the menu?

5 I met any really interesting people at the conference.

6 Product quality is very good – we don't have some serious complaints.

7 Some countries in Sub-Saharan Africa have a lot of precious metals.

8 Mali and Chad don't have some precious metals.

41.2 Complete the sentences with *some* or *any*.

1 There are _____ colours that we never use for our products – pink for example.

2 You can have _____ colour – bright pink, lime green, deep purple, whatever.

3 Choose _____ design you want – they are all the same price.

4 Choose carefully – _____ designs are a little more expensive.

41.3 <u>Underline</u> the correct word.

1 *How many/How much* work do you do with corporate clients?

2 *How many/How much* employees work here at Head Office?

3 I spoke with *a few/a little* colleagues about it.

4 I have *a few/a little* information about their company, but not much.

5 Japan doesn't have *much/many* oil, gas or coal.

6 Japan doesn't have *much/many* natural resources.

7 We're paying *a lot of/much* money for their services.

41.4 Complete the dialogue with these words: *much, many, a little, a few*.

DEXTER: You work for one of those big, old-fashioned telecoms companies, right? It can't be easy. How (1) _____ profit do you make from your fixed-line voice business these days? Take me as an example. I only make (2) _____ calls from the fixed line in my office – most of the time I use my cell phone.

GEETA: Hold on just a minute. You're right that we don't have (3) _____ opportunities to grow the traditional business, but that's not where our profits come from. They come from broadband: Internet access, voice-over-Internet services, digital media. We only need (4) _____ time and then we'll dominate the market again like we did in the eighties and nineties.

"I like to keep a few pictures of my loved ones on my desk."

42 Determiners 2

A All

● After *all*, study when we can and cannot leave out the word *of*.

before *the* or *this*:   **All (of) the** *work is seasonal.*
before a possessive adjective *(my/our/your)*:   **All (of) my** *friends work in the media.*
before a pronoun *(it/us/you)*:   *I didn't read* **all of it**. (but NOT ~~all it~~)

Compare with other words like *most/many/some* where we never leave out *of*:

Most of the work is seasonal.   (NOT ~~most the work~~)
Some of my friends work in the media.   (NOT ~~some my friends~~)

● We do not normally use *all* on its own as a single-word noun. Instead we use *everyone* or *everything*.

Everyone agreed with my proposal.   (NOT ~~All agreed with my proposal.~~)
Everything is going well.   (NOT ~~All is going well.~~)

B No/none

● We use *no* where a noun (or adjective + noun) follows immediately.

***No worker/No unskilled worker** has a permanent contract.*

But we use *none of* where a noun does not follow immediately.

***None of** <u>the</u> workers/<u>our</u> workers/<u>them</u> has a permanent contract.*

● We do not use double negatives (two negative words in the same sentence). Instead, we use *any*.

*I haven't seen **any** jobs advertised at IBM recently.*   (NOT ~~I haven't seen no jobs~~)
*I've **never** seen **any** jobs advertised at IBM.*   (NOT ~~I've never seen no jobs~~)

C Each/every

● *Each* and *every* have a similar meaning. They are both used with a singular noun.

***Each/every employee** receives a small gift at Christmas.*   (NOT ~~every employees~~)

● For small numbers *each* is more usual, and for two of something we must use *each*.

*I interviewed three candidates, and **each** one had different strengths and weaknesses.*
*He had a bag in **each** hand.*

● We can say *each of*, but we cannot say *every of*.

*The hotel has forty rooms, and **each of** them has a sea view.*

D Both/either/neither

Both   ☑ ☑   ***Both** my parents are doctors.*
Either   ☑ ☒ / ☒ ☑   *Coke or Pepsi? I don't mind, **either one** is OK.*
Neither ☒ ☒   *The two companies merged – **neither one** could survive on its own.*

● Note that when we have two choices we say *either ... or ...*, (NOT ~~or ... or ...~~)

*We can **either** take the train **or** catch a taxi.* (NOT ~~or take the train~~)

Exercises

42.1 <u>Underline</u> the correct words.

1 The trade fair is very important – the boss wants *all us/all of us* on the stand.

2 *All the sales reps/Most the sales reps* have to work on the stand.

3 *Some of countries/Some countries* have imposed import restrictions.

4 *All/Everything* is automated in our factory nowadays.

5 We're lucky – *none of files/none of the files* have been corrupted by the virus.

6 There were *none messages/no messages* on my voicemail.

7 I don't see *any end/no end* to the fall in the dollar.

8 I think we've explored *every option/every options*.

9 Silvio, Leonora and Daniele all spoke in the meeting, and *each one/every one* had a different point of view.

10 I can't come at the weekend. I'm busy *both days/every day*.

11 It was an amazing experience – *either of us/neither of us* will forget it.

12 You can pay *or/either* by credit card or in cash.

42.2 Fill each gap with one word so that both sentences have a similar meaning.

1 The hotels are both unsuitable.

    Neither hotel *is* suitable.

2 All the customers are complaining about the price increase.

    _____ customer _____ complaining about the price increase.

3 No customers are complaining about the price increase.

    _____ _____ the customers are complaining about the price increase.

4 There were no attachments with your email.

    There weren't _____ attachments with your email.

5 Singapore and Hong Kong too are key financial centres in South East Asia.

    Singapore and Hong Kong – _____ are key financial centres in South East Asia.

6 Singapore or Hong Kong could dominate the financial world.

    Singapore or Hong Kong – _____ one could dominate the financial world.

42.3 Complete the text with these words: *both, each, either, neither, no, none.*

Portugal and Greece: new opportunities

Portugal and Greece are similar in many respects. (1) _____ countries joined the European Union in the 1980s, and with EU subsidies (2) _____ one made considerable progress. But those subsidies are ending, and (3) _____ country will find the future so easy. What opportunities are there? Portugal could take advantage of its historical links to countries like Brazil, Angola and Mozambique that speak Portuguese – although (4) _____ of these are in the EU. Greece could increase trade with its regional partners, (5) _____ Turkey or the Balkan states. But one thing is clear: there are (6) _____ easy solutions.

A   *A* or *an*?

● We say *a* before consonant sounds, and *an* before vowel sounds.

consonant sounds   ***a** company,* ***a** product,* ***a** euro,* ***a** unit*
vowel sounds   ***an** agenda,* ***an** organization,* ***an** hour,* ***an** MBA*

B   Uses of *a/an*

● We use *a* or *an* to mean *one*.

*I get over **a** hundred emails every day.*   (a hundred / a thousand / a million)

● We use *a* or *an* when we mention a person or thing for the first time.

*I'm going for **an interview** at Siemens next week.*

● We use *a* or *an* when the person or thing we are talking about is not specific.

*We need to call **a** technician.* (any technician, not one particular person)

● We use *a* or *an* to say what job someone does.

*Anne is **a** lawyer.*

● We use *a* or *an* to talk about frequency. *Per* can also be used.

*once **a/per** year   500 units **a/per** day   we charge €200 **an/per** hour*

C   Uses of *the*

● We use *the* when it is clear which person or thing we are talking about.

a) It is clear because the person or thing has already been mentioned.

*We need **a meeting**. **The meeting** should cover the questions of cost and timing.*

b) It is clear from the context (even though we are mentioning it for the first time).

***The** situation needs to be monitored carefully.*

c) It is clear because there is only one.

*I was speaking to **the** Sales Director about their new product.*

D   *A* or *the*?

● In general we use *a/an* for introducing new information.

*I have **a suggestion** to make.*
*I'm not unemployed any more. I've started **a business** of my own.*

We use *the* for referring to something that the listener already knows about.

***The suggestion** you made at the last meeting was very interesting.*
***The business** we are in is very competitive.*

● With uncountable nouns we do not use *a/an*. We use *the* or *some*.

*Can you give me **the/some information**?*   (NOT ~~an information~~)
*This report is about **the/some research** we're doing.* (NOT ~~a research~~)

"Somewhere out there, Patrick, is the key to increased sales. I want you to find that key, Patrick, and bring it to me."

Exercises

43.1 <u>Underline</u> the correct words. In each sentence, one answer is *a/an* and one is *the*.

1 There's *a/the* man waiting for you in *a/the* reception area.

2 *A/The* man we met yesterday has sent us *an/the* email asking about our services.

3 It was *a/the* good meeting, but I had to leave early. What happened at *an/the* end?

4 I had *a/the* great holiday. *A/The* weather was perfect.

5 *A/The* Customer Services department receives over 100 calls *a/the* day.

6 Can I give you *a/the* lift to *a/the* airport?

48

43.2 In each A/B mini-dialogue, fill in one gap with *a/an* and one with *the*.

1 A: I emailed you on Friday with __*an*__ order for 2,000 units of your new video game. Our reference number was AJ946. Did you receive it?

   B: Yes, madam, _____ order is being shipped today.

2 A: Things are difficult right now. There must be a way out of _____ situation.

   B: You're right, although it's not _____ situation I've ever been in before.

3 A: This contract is really confusing. We need the advice of _____ lawyer.

   B: Yes, but which one? _____ lawyer we used last time was really expensive.

4 A: Have you got _____ new password they gave us to log on to the network?

   B: I'll have a look. I've got _____ password written down somewhere, but I think it's one of the old ones.

43.3 In each sentence, fill in one gap with *a/an* and one with *the*.

1 Baljeet is _____ accountant. He works on _____ fourth floor.

2 _____ presentation you gave yesterday was _____ great success.

3 Where is _____ report we were looking at? It was on my desk _____ hour ago.

4 We're thinking of buying _____ new photocopier for _____ whole department.

5 _____ research we do in our labs is _____ very important factor in our success.

6 Ilona works in _____ hotel. You know, _____ one opposite the station.

49

43.4 Complete the text with *a/an* (4 times) or *the* (4 times).

Come to Singapore!

Why choose Singapore? Singapore is (1) _____ nation that welcomes investors both large and small, and already more than 7,000 companies from around (2) _____ world have set up offices there. Singapore's location is perfect: there are 2.8 billion people no more than (3) _____ seven-hour flight away. These people live in fast-growing markets with (4) _____ enormous appetite for consumer goods. In Singapore (5) _____ political and social environment is stable, and (6) _____ lifestyle is good too. It's (7) _____ shopper's paradise, and (8) _____ food is superb.

A *The*/no article

● We use *the* when we are talking about specific things. We use no article when we are talking generally. Compare:

*I sent **the invoices** this morning.*   (the listener knows which invoices)
***Invoices** must be paid within 30 days.*   (invoices in general, not any specific ones)
*I work in **the insurance business**.*   (we know which business)
***Business** is going well at the moment.*   (business in general, not any specific areas)
*Thank you for **the information**.*   (the listener knows which information)
***Information** is power.*   (information in general)

● We use no article for most companies.

***Microsoft** and **Google** dominate the online search business.*

● We use no article for languages.

I can speak English and French. (NOT ~~the English and the French~~)

B Special uses of *the*

● We use *the* with superlatives. (See unit 49.)

*Sony is **the biggest** brand name in consumer electronics.*
*We only use **the best** quality ingredients in our food.*

● We use *the* with nationalities.

*In my experience, **the Portuguese** and **the Dutch** are very good negotiators.*

C Place names: no article and *the*

● We use no article for most geographical place names: continents, countries, states, single islands, cities, roads, mountains and lakes.

Europe/Asia   France/Slovenia   California/Yorkshire   Malta/Taiwan
Tokyo/Prague   Fifth Avenue/Piccadilly   Mont Blanc/Mount Everest   Lake Geneva/Lake Baikal

● We use *the* for oceans, seas, rivers and canals.
***the** Pacific, **the** Mediterranean, **the** Rhine/**the** Amazon, **the** Suez Canal*

● We use *the* for republics, states and kingdoms:
***the** Czech Republic, **the** United States, **the** United Kingdom*

● We use *the* for plural names:
***the** Netherlands, **the** Bahamas, **the** Alps*

● We use *the* with *of*: ***the** South of France* BUT *Southern France* (no article).

● With buildings, we use
the for famous buildings: ***the** Taj Mahal, **the** Petronas Twin Towers, **the** Eiffel Tower*
the for hotels: ***the** Hilton, **the** Ritz*
no article if there is a place name: *Shanghai International Airport, Cologne Cathedral*

Exercises

44.1 Each pair has one right and one wrong sentence. Tick (✓) the right sentence.

1   a) In business, time is money. ✓
    b) We should have a good profit when we've received all money from TransCo.

2   a) The shares in my portfolio have performed well over the last year.
    b) The shares can be a risky investment.

3   a) Profits we made last quarter were up by 4% on the quarter before.
    b) Profits are increasing in all of our major markets.

4   a) Don't worry about him – the people can be very strange sometimes.
    b) I really like the people in my office – we all get along very well.

5   a) I'm a vegetarian; I don't eat meat.
    b) Meat I had at lunchtime was delicious.

6   a) The management has offered the workers a 3% pay rise.
    b) The management is an art, not a science.

7   a) People in the French Revolution wanted 'Liberty, Equality, Fraternity'.
    b) People in the French Revolution wanted 'The liberty, The equality, The fraternity'.

Now correct the wrong sentences by adding or removing the word *the*.

44.2 Tick (✓) two sentences that are right. Add the word *the* to two sentences.

1   English are famous for their sense of humour, but not for their cooking.
2   I've been studying English for three years, and I'm slowly making progress.
3   Time magazine said most important person of the last century was Albert Einstein.
4   In the Time magazine opinion poll, most people voted for Albert Einstein.

44.3 Complete the text by writing *the* or ~ (if there is no article).

An Economist Intelligence Unit report showed that in 2004 the fastest growing countries in (1) ____ Europe were (2) ____ Republic of Ireland and (3) ____ United Kingdom, and the slowest growing were (4) ____ Germany and (5) ____ Netherlands.

50

44.4 Complete the text by writing *the* or ~ (if there is no article).

Oil and tourism in the Strait of Hormuz

About 25% of the world's oil production passes through a narrow channel of water off the coast of (1) ____ Iran called (2) ____ Strait of Hormuz. It is the entrance to (3) ____ Indian Ocean for oil tankers coming from countries such as (4) ____ Iraq and (5) ____ United Arab Emirates. Near the coast is an interesting island called (6) ____ Kish. The Iranian government is developing it as a luxury tourist destination, with a 7-star hotel to rival (7) ____ Burj al-Arab Hotel in Dubai. Project managers are (8) ____ Drees & Sommer AG, a German company.

Possessives

A Possessive adjectives and pronouns

Subject	*I*	*you*	*he*	*she*	*it*	*we*	*they*
Possessive adjective	*my*	*your*	*his*	*her*	*its*	*our*	*their*
Possessive pronoun	*mine*	*yours*	*his*	*hers*	*~*	*ours*	*theirs*

● Possessive adjectives are used before a noun.

  *I'd like you to meet **my colleague**. **Her name** is Roberta.*
  *Switzerland is famous for **its banks** and **its chocolate**.*

● We can use *own* after a possessive adjective.

  *I don't have **my own apartment** – I'm staying with some friends.*

● Possessive pronouns stand on their own. They are not used before a noun.

  *Here come the starters – the soup is **mine** and the carpaccio is **yours**.*

● Note the relation between a possessive adjective and a possessive pronoun.

  *This is **my office**. This office is **mine**.*
  *It's **our future**. The future is **ours**.*

● Note that there is no apostrophe in possessive adjectives and possessive pronouns ending in *-s*.

  (NOT Switzerland is famous for ~~it's banks~~.)
  (NOT The future is ~~our's~~.)

B 's (apostrophe s)

● We use apostrophe *s* (*'s*) to show possession: something belongs to a person, organization, country, etc. Many other languages use *of* in these cases. We use *'s* even if the name ends in *-s*.

  Linda's suggestion   Russia's oil reserves
  Charles's office   The boss's office

● With a plural noun we add the apostrophe only.

  The attached document lists all our customers' account details.

● We can use the *'s* form without a following noun if the meaning is clear.

  This is my office, and that one is Annette's.

● Note that *'s* can also be a contraction of *is* or *has*.

  ***It's** an interesting suggestion.*   *(It's = It is)*
  ***It's** been a pleasure meeting you.*   *(It's = It has)*

C A friend of mine, etc

● When we describe the relationship between people, we often use *of* with a possessive form.

  of + possessive pronoun: *I met a colleague **of yours** at the conference.*
  of + apostrophe: *Nick is a friend **of my brother's**.*

Exercises

45.1 <u>Underline</u> the correct words.

1 Excuse me, I think those are <u>our</u>/ours seats.

2 Excuse me, I think those seats are our/ours.

3 I can never remember where I put my/mine car in the airport car park.

4 Where's my car? Oh, there it is – that one's my/mine.

5 Versace's new range is fabulous – have you seen their/theirs magazine advert?

6 This is my copy of the agenda, and this is your/yours.

7 As a freelancer, I do all my/mine own book-keeping.

8 Is this pen yours/your's or mine?

9 India is improving its/it's infrastructure to attract new businesses.

10 Jane will be here in a moment – she's talking to a friend of her/hers.

45.2 Complete the sentences with these words: *her, hers, their, theirs, your, yours.*

1 Coca-Cola sell sweet, fizzy water. What is the secret of _____ success?

2 Our photocopier isn't working, but the sales department say we can use _____

3 It's up to you. The decision is _____

4 It's up to you. It's _____ decision.

5 Ask Mary if these keys are _____

6 The strongest candidate is Sylvia Poggioli – here is _____ CV.

45.3 Tick (✓) the correct box, to show how *'s* is being used.

	possession	's = is	's = has
1 Ingrid's an excellent conference presenter.	☐	☐	☐
2 Ingrid's conference presentation was excellent.	☐	☐	☐
3 Ingrid's given several presentations this year.	☐	☐	☐

45.4 In this email, add *'s* (apostrophe s) in seven places, and add *s* (s on its own) in two places.

Subject Frankfurt Trade Fair

Felix – it time to start planning the Frankfurt Trade Fair. I thought I'd start by looking at last year report, which was written by Lena. It says that our stand was very attractive visually, but our main competitor stand had more people working on it, giving out brochures, etc. In terms of numbers, their stand was visited by approximately 20% more people than our. Lena organized everything last time, but this year she very busy, and anyway I think it someone else turn, not her. What about Andreas Kofler from the Stuttgart office? Andreas input to the planning of the sales conference last March was very good – should we ask him to take responsibility?

Pronouns

*Airlines: Reinvent **yourselves**
or disappear*

Forrester website

A **Reflexive pronouns: *myself/ourselves***

Singular	*myself*	*yourself*	*himself/herself/itself*
Plural	*ourselves*	*yourselves*	*themselves*

● Note that there is a plural *you* form.

● We use a reflexive pronoun when the object is the same as the subject. Compare:

I've cut the cake into twelve pieces.	*I cut **myself** while I was shaving.*
We enjoyed the trip to Vienna.	*We enjoyed **ourselves** on the trip to Vienna.*
I think I hurt her feelings yesterday.	*I hurt **myself** on the ski slopes at Klosters.*
Heidi introduced me to her boss.	***Heidi** introduced **herself** to me.*
I saw your presentation on video.	*I hate to see **myself** on video.*

● Note the expression for offering something: *Help yourself to …*

● The following verbs are usually not reflexive in English: *change* (clothes), *complain, decide, dress, feel, meet, relax, remember, rest, sit down, stand up, wake up, wash, worry.*

When I sit on the beach I can really relax. (NOT ~~relax myself~~)
How do you feel? Are you OK? (NOT ~~How do you feel yourself?~~)
I woke up, washed, and dressed for work. (NOT ~~woke up myself, washed myself,~~ etc)

● We can also use *by* + reflexive pronoun to mean 'without help'.

*Richard Branson set up Virgin Atlantic Airways (by) **himself**.*

*Welcome to Online
Conversion.com – Convert just
about **anything** to **anything**
else. Length/Distance,
Temperature, Speed, More…*

OnlineConversion.com website

B **Indefinite pronouns: *someone/everyone***

● Words like *everyone, anything* are called indefinite pronouns. They refer to people, things or places without saying exactly who, what or where they are.

people	*someone*	*anyone*	*everyone*	*no one (or no-one)*
	somebody	*anybody*	*everybody*	*nobody*
things	*something*	*anything*	*everything*	*nothing*
places	*somewhere*	*anywhere*	*everywhere*	*nowhere*

● *some-* is common in affirmative sentences, *any-* is common in questions and negatives.

*I'd like to talk to you about **something**.* (affirmative)
*I **don't** know **anything** about it. Do you know **anything**?* (negative/question)

● We can use *some* in a question if it is an offer or request.

*Can I ask you **something**?*

● We can use *any* in an affirmative sentence if the meaning is 'no limit'.

*Walk **anywhere** you want on the construction site, as long as you're careful.*

● Double negatives are not used, instead we use *any*.

*I've tried calling them, but there **isn't any**one there.* (NOT ~~there isn't no one there~~)

● These rules are the same as those in unit 41.

"And now at this point in the meeting I'd like to shift the blame away from me and onto someone else."

Exercises

46.1 <u>Underline</u> the correct words.

1   It's very heavy! Be careful when you lift it. Don't *hurt/<u>hurt yourself</u>*.

2   I need to go back to the hotel to *change/change myself* before dinner.

3   I might go home early today. I *feel/feel myself* ill.

4   It was a great holiday. We really *enjoyed/enjoyed ourselves*.

5   Thank you for coming to the interview. Please *sit down/sit down yourself*.

6   I never went to English classes – I *taught/taught myself* just by using books.

7   It's time for a break. Please *help/help yourselves* to more coffee.

8   The food was so bad that I *complained/complained myself* to the waiter.

9   I'm tired – I *woke up/woke up myself* at 5 am when the baby started crying.

10 Let me *introduce/introduce myself*. My name is Liu Mingkang.

46.2 The indefinite pronoun is wrong in each sentence. Cross it out and correct it.

1   I didn't make a back-up copy. It's my fault and I can't blame ~~no one~~ else.   *anyone*

2   We forgot about refreshments. There's *anything* for our visitors to eat or drink!

3   I've looked *anywhere*, but I can't find the recharger for my cell phone.

4   Emma and I have worked together for years. *Someone* knows her better than me.

5   *Anyone* called you earlier, but they didn't leave a message.

6   The server has crashed and there isn't *nothing* we can do until tomorrow.

7   You can do *something* you want. It makes no difference to me.

8   The weather was awful. It snowed overnight and *anyone* was late for work.

51 **46.3** Complete the dialogue with these words: *anything, everything, nothing, something*.

ANGELIKA: Sales are down again this year in Latin America. It's a disaster. Since the merger
(1) _____ has gone right.

MICHAEL: There must be (2) _____ we can do.

ANGELIKA: But what? There isn't (3) _____ else. We've tried (4) _____

52 **46.4** Complete the dialogue with these words: *anyone, everyone, no one, someone*.

SINEAD: I couldn't get to the meeting yesterday – (1) _____ called with a problem that I had
to deal with. What did people think about Marta's proposal to license our software? Did
(2) _____ argue against it?

RADU: No, not really. Basically, (3) _____ thought it was a really good idea. There
were a few questions about the legal details, but (4) _____ argued against it.

47 *It's* and *there's*

A *It* as an 'empty' subject with no meaning

- We use *it* as an 'empty' subject (it has no meaning) in these cases:

times, days, dates	*It's one o'clock. It's Tuesday. It's July 28.*
weather, temperature	*It's a beautiful day. It rained all night. It's 30 degrees.*
distances	*It's about five kilometres from here to our factory.*
general situation	*What's it like working for an American company?*

- We also use *it* as an 'empty' subject in these expressions:

It's + adjective + that	*It's nice/strange/interesting that ...*
It's + adjective + to	*It's important/essential/nice to ...*
It looks/seems/appears	*It looks/seems like we're not going to get the contract.*
	It looks/seems as if we're not going to get the contract.
	It seems/appears (that) we're not going to get the contract.

- Remember that *it* also refers back to something already mentioned.

  This is the new model. It's on sale for €290.

B *There's ...* to say that something exists

- We use *there is* and *there are* to say that something exists.

  There's *a package for you in reception.*
  There are *five sales reps in my team.*
  Is there *time to look round the factory?*
  There aren't *enough photocopies.*

- Note these other structures with *there*.

There + modal + be	*There could/may/shouldn't be a problem.*
There seems/appears to be	*There seems/appears to be a mistake in the invoice.*

C *There is/we have/we've got*

- We can often use *we have* or *we've got* in place of *there is*.

  There's/We have/We've got *a package for you in reception.*
  Is there/Do we have/Have we got *time to look round the factory?*
  There aren't/We don't have/We haven't got *enough photocopies.*

- Compare *have* and *have got*:

  I have a BMW.   I don't have enough time.   Do you have my number?
  I've got a BMW.   I haven't got enough time.   Have you got my number?

  The meaning is the same. *Have got* is more informal and we usually use contractions. *Have got* is particularly common in British English.

SO WE'RE AGREED THEN THERE'S NO NEED TO MAKE ANY CHANGES TO OUR EQUAL OPPORTUNITIES EMPLOYMENT POLICIES

IF IT AIN'T BROKE WHY FIX IT?

IT'S ALWAYS WORKED FOR ME!

Exercises

47.1 Put one of these in each space: *it, it's, there, there's, there are.*

1 <u>*There's*</u> a champagne reception after the product launch. <u>*It*</u> begins at 5 pm.
2 _____ strange that _____ no figures for the current quarter in this report.
3 _____ looks as if _____ may be a delay shipping these parts.
4 _____ must be another solution to this problem. I'm sure _____ other ways to approach this that we haven't considered yet.
5 _____ incredible that _____ still no fall in the bond market.
6 _____ seems to be a misunderstanding here. _____ looks like they've given us a quotation for the wrong product.
7 Right next to the conference centre _____ a little Italian restaurant. _____ opened this year.
8 Thanks for calling. _____ always good to hear from you, and _____ one or two things we need to discuss.
9 _____ important to remember that _____ many other advertising agencies we could use.
10 Hi Ingrid. Sorry I haven't written for so long. How's _____ going? Here in Helsinki _____ the beginning of winter. _____ white clouds in the sky and _____ looks like _____ going to snow.

47.2 Complete the conversation. Use the words in brackets in the correct form. Use contractions where possible.

LISA: Claude, (1) <u>*have you got*</u> (you/got) a moment? I've been trying to speak to you all morning but you're always on the phone!

CLAUDE : Of course. I'm not too busy right now, although (2) _____ (I/got) a meeting at three o'clock. (3) _____ (there/be) a problem?

LISA : No, (4) _____ (there/not/be) anything to worry about.

CLAUDE : I hope it's not that customer from Manchester again. (5) _____ (there/be) always something about his phone calls that gives me a headache.

LISA : Yes, it is him. Someone needs to call him this afternoon. Natalia was going to do it, but (6) _____ (she/got) a doctor's appointment, and (7) _____ (I/not/have) all the details of the case.

CLAUDE : OK, I'll do it. (8) _____ (you/got) his file?

LISA : File? What file? (9) _____ (I/not/got) a file. (10) _____ (there/be) some files on the floor by Natalia's desk – perhaps it's one of those.

CLAUDE : I knew this afternoon was going to be difficult.

48 Adjectives and adverbs

A Introduction

- Adjectives describe nouns, and come before them.

  *There was **slow growth** in our market share last year.*

  Adverbs describe verbs, and come after them.

  *Last year our market share **grew slowly**.*

- We usually form adverbs by adding *-ly* to an adjective. Sometimes we add *-y*, *-ally*, or *-ily*, depending on the spelling of the original adjective.

  *slow – slow**ly***   *quick – quick**ly***   *careful – careful**ly***   *full – ful**ly***
  *dramatic – dramatic**ally***   *heavy – heav**ily***

- Some adjectives and adverbs have the same form.

  early   fast   hard   late   high   low   right   daily/weekly/monthly/quarterly

  *We can usually make a **fast** decision.*   *This model is selling very **fast**.*
  *You've made the **right** choice.*   *The machine isn't working **right**.*

- Some adjectives already end in *-ly*, and have no corresponding adverb. Examples are: *friendly, lonely, silly, costly.*

B Verb + adjective

- Some verbs are followed by an adjective (without a noun) rather than an adverb. These include: *appear, be, become, feel, look, seem, smell, taste, sound.*

  *The new brochure **looks fantastic**.*   (NOT ~~fantastically~~)
  *She **sounded angry** when she called.*   (NOT ~~angrily~~)

C Good/well

- *Good* is an adjective. *Well* is an adverb.

  *Pele was a **good footballer**.*   (adjective + noun)
  *Pele **played** football **well**.*   (verb + adverb)

D Order of adverbs

- An adverb can be a word or a phrase. It says how (*carefully/little by little*), where (*there/in the French market*) or when (*yesterday/last year*) something happens.

- 'How' and 'Where' adverbs usually come after the verb.

  *We **planned** the product launch very **carefully**.*
  *We **launched** the new model **in the French market**.*

- 'When' adverbs can come before or after the verb.

  ***Last week** we **planned** the product launch.*
  *We **planned** the product launch **last week**.*

- If we have several adverbs, the usual order is: HOW – WHERE – WHEN.

  *Our sales rose **significantly in China last year**.* (NOT ~~last year in China~~)

Exercises

48.1 Compete the second sentence with a verb + adverb. The verbs are in the past simple.

1   There was a gradual improvement in sales last quarter.
    Last quarter sales ____*improved gradually.*____

2   There was a slow recovery in the economy last year.
    Last year the economy _____

3   There was a dramatic collapse in their share price because of the scandal.
    Because of the scandal, their share price _____

4   There was a slight increase in unemployment last month.
    Last month unemployment _____

48.2 Underline the correct words. The answers are all adverbs.

1   We don't have much time. The deadline is approaching very *quick/quickly*.
2   We don't have much time. The deadline is approaching very *fast/fastly*.
3   I arrived *late/lately*, and the meeting had already started.
4   I arrived *unexpected/unexpectedly*, and the meeting had already started.
5   The whole team has worked very *efficient/efficiently*.
6   The whole team has worked very *hard/hardly*.

48.3 Put the underlined adverbs in each sentence into the correct order.

1   The demand for oil is growing right now all over the world considerably.
2   She's done in her career well in recent years.

48.4 In each sentence, fill in one gap with *good* and one with *well*.

1   Don't worry, I know him very _____ . He's a _____ person.
2   This candidate has a _____ CV, and she says she speaks German _____
3   The company is not doing _____ . This is not a _____ time to buy their shares.

48.5 Choose either an adjective or an adverb from the words in *italics*.

BOSE: AUDIO TECHNOLOGY AT ITS BEST

Bose is one of the most (1) *important/importantly* names in audio technology, and is well-known for investing (2) *heavy/heavily* in research and development. Their home music systems look (3) *great/greatly* and sound (4) *fantastic/fantastically*, but this (5) *high/highly* performance is achieved in units with a very small size. In the automobile industry, certain makes of car have Bose sound systems that are designed (6) *specific/specifically* to fit the acoustics of the car's interior. And Bose headphones reproduce (7) *exact/exactly* the same sound as your living-room system, even though they are so (8) *light/lightly*.

54

Comparison 1: adjectives

A Comparatives and superlatives

- We use the comparative form of an adjective to compare two separate things.

  *Argentina has **a bigger** economy **than** Chile.*   (note the use of *than*)

- We use the superlative form to compare one thing in a group with all the others.

  *Brazil has **the biggest** economy in Latin America.*   (note the use of *the*)

B Form: short and long adjectives

- The comparative and superlative form of an adjective depends on whether it is short or long (the number of syllables in the word) and its spelling.

Short adjectives			
	adjective	comparative	superlative
regular	cheap	cheaper	the cheapest
	small	smaller	the smallest
ending in one vowel + one consonant: double consonant	hot	hotter	the hottest
	big	bigger	the biggest
ending in –y: change to *i*	dry	drier	the driest
irregular forms	good	better	the best
	bad	worse	the worst
	far	further	the furthest

*UBS is a **large** bank, although HSBC is **larger than** UBS. Citigroup is **the largest** bank in the world.*

Long adjectives		
adjective	comparative	superlative
modern	**more/less** modern	**the most/the least** modern
interesting	**more/less** interesting	**the most/the least** interesting

*Seiko watches are **expensive**, although Rolex are **more expensive than** Seiko.*
*Patek Philippe are **the most expensive** watches in the world.*

"Honesty is the best policy, Fernbaugh, but it's not company policy."

C Other structures: *as ... as .../more and more ...*

- We can also make comparisons with *as ... as* and *not as ... as*.

  *Kentucky Fried Chicken in China is nearly **as profitable as** in the United States.*
  *Cisco's third quarter profit was **not as large as** Wall Street expected.*

- We can describe a trend using *-er* and *-er* or *more and more*.

  *It's **harder and harder** to make a profit in the music business.*
  *It's **more and more difficult** to make a profit in the music business.*

Exercises

49.1 Complete the table.

	Adjective	Comparative	Superlative
1	expensive	more expensive than	the most expensive
2	_____	_____	the most profitable
3	_____	safer than	_____
4	_____	_____	the biggest
5	risky	_____	_____
6	_____	better than	_____
7	_____	worse than	_____
8	powerful	_____	_____
9	new	_____	_____
10	_____	further than	_____

49.2 Underline the correct words.

1 New York is *the most exciting/the most excitingest* city I know.

2 Nothing is *worse/worst* than missing a flight because of the traffic.

3 It's getting *each time more/more and more* common to make calls over the Net.

4 What! €600! That's a lot of money. It's *more/most* expensive than I expected.

5 €500 is a lot, but I knew it would cost that. *It's/It isn't* as expensive as I expected.

6 Only €400! That's good. *It's/It isn't* as expensive as I expected.

55

49.3 Complete the text by putting the adjectives in brackets into the correct form. There are seven comparatives, four superlatives, and one answer that needs *as*.

Apple: the story continues

From success to near failure and back to success. Of all the turnaround stories in the business world, perhaps Apple is the (1)___*most famous*___ (famous). In the early 1980s, Apple computers were (2) _____ (fast) and (3) _____ (functional) than IBM computers, who were the (4) _____ (close) competitor. But in 1985 IBM shipped a computer using the Microsoft Windows operating system for the first time, and this made it nearly (5) _____ (good) as an Apple. Apple was in trouble, especially when Microsoft developed a business strategy that was much (6) _____ (successful) than their own. Microsoft decided that it would license Windows to a variety of different PC makers, not just IBM. As a result, Windows became the industry standard, and Apple's market share became (7) _____ (small) and (8) _____ (small). But Apple wasn't finished. In 1997 they brought back Steve Jobs, the founder of the company. He concentrated on design, and Mac computers became (9) _____ (trendy) and (10) _____ (exciting) than boring PCs. But Steve Jobs' (11) _____ (great) success was in 2001, when Apple launched the iPod – the (12) _____ (cool) music player the world had ever seen.

A Comparing adverbs

● In general, adverbs follow the same rules as adjectives. (See unit 49.)

	Adverb	**Comparative**	**Superlative**
short adverbs	*fast*	*faster*	*the fastest*
ending in –*y*	*early*	*earlier*	*the earliest*
longer adverbs	*efficiently*	*more/less efficiently*	*the most/least efficiently*

*At the factory in China we can produce the goods **more cheaply than** in Mexico.*
*The person who arrives at the office **the earliest** is Sonia.*

● The adverbs *well* and *badly* are irregular.

well **better** **the best**   *badly* **worse** **the worst**

*In the autumn, light-coloured coats sell **well**, although brown coats sell **better**. Black coats sell **the best** because people can wear them all through the winter.*

B Comparing nouns

● We use different words for countable and uncountable nouns. (See unit 39.)

The EU would like to divert as much cargo as possible from roads to railways.

Slovenia Business Week website

Countable nouns	
comparative	**superlative**
more/fewer/(not) as many as	the most/the fewest

*We have **more clients** in Germany and Switzerland than in the rest of Europe.*
*We've had **fewer complaints** since we improved our quality control system.*
*A fuel cell power system doesn't have **as many** moving **parts as** a regular engine.*

Uncountable nouns	
comparative	**superlative**
more/less/(not) as much as	the most/the least

*Ask Linda – she has **more knowledge** of the US market than me.*
*If you become a freelancer, you'll earn **less money**.*
*We don't have **as much information as** we need.*

C Large and small differences

*In the EU, unemployment stood at 8.9% in March, **slightly lower** than the 9.0% registered in March last year.*

Industry Week website

● Here are the prices of four products:

Product A €200   Product B €250   Product C €400   Product D €450

● Study how we can talk about large and small differences:

*Product B is **a bit more/slightly more** expensive than product A.*
*Product C is **much more/a lot more** expensive than product A.*
*Product D is **far more** expensive than product A.*

● We can use *almost, (not) nearly, twice* with the structure *as … as.*

*Product C is **almost/nearly** as expensive <u>as</u> product D.*
*Product B is **not nearly** as expensive <u>as</u> product D.*
*Product C is **twice** <u>as</u> expensive <u>as</u> product A.*

Exercises

50.1 <u>Underline</u> the correct words.

1   I'm sorry, the meeting took *longer than/the longest* I expected.

2   The line is bad – could you speak *more louder/more loudly* please?

3   With this new software tool, you can work *more efficiently/more efficienter*.

4   The Russian economy is performing *better/more better* this year.

5   This year our raw materials cost nearly *the double/twice as much* money.

6   Our raw materials cost nearly twice as much money *than/as* last year.

56 **50.2** Complete this voicemail using these words: *more, fewer, less, as many, as much.*

> Celine, I wanted to let you know about the two candidates I interviewed for the job of regional sales manager. Their names were Yvette Ferrand and Elene Briel.
>
> Yvette has several positive points: she has (1) _____ experience of international markets than Elene, and so it would take (2) _____ time to train her. On the negative side, she doesn't have (3) _____ experience of the fashion business as I would like – her background is more in cosmetics. Also, her only foreign language is English, so she doesn't speak (4) _____ languages as Elene.
>
> Elene speaks German and Spanish as well as English. Elene's other strong point is that she would be more committed to the company. She has changed jobs (5) _____ times than Yvette, who seems to move on to a new job every two years.
>
> I think we need a meeting before we can decide, and possibly a final interview with both candidates. When are you free?

57 **50.3** Complete this report using these words: *much, not nearly, slightly, twice.*

> ### REPORT: LOCATION OF NEW OFFICES
>
> The Board asked me to prepare a report comparing two different options for our new offices. Please refer to the table as you read this summary:
>
> | | size | rent | renovation costs |
> | --- | --- | --- | --- |
> | Building A: city centre | 1,000m^2 | €400/m^2 | €600,000 |
> | Building B: suburbs | 1,050m^2 | €200/m^2 | €150,000 |
>
> The two buildings are more or less the same size, although building B is (1) _____ bigger. Our current offices are just 600m^2, so in either case we would have (2) _____ more space than now. There is a big difference in rental costs, as Building A is in the city centre. In fact, at €400 per square metre the rent there is (3) _____ as expensive. Building A has another disadvantage – it's quite old and would need about €600,000 to renovate and refurbish it before we could move in. The work required in Building B is (4) _____ as much, only €150,000.

 **Degree**

A Too/not enough

● *Too* means 'more than is necessary or good'. *Not enough* means 'less than is necessary or good'. Both suggest that there is a problem.

adjectives	*We can't accept your proposal – the price is **too high**.*
	*We can't accept your proposal – the price is**n't low enough**.*
adverbs	*He speaks **too quickly** and it's hard to understand him.*
	*He doesn't speak **slowly enough** and it's hard to understand him.*
nouns: countable	*There are **too many details** in this report. It needs to be shorter.*
	*There aren't **enough details** in this report. It needs to be longer.*
nouns: uncountable	*There is **too much information** in this report.*
	*There isn't **enough information** in this report.*

● Note the position of *enough* in the examples above: after adjectives (*low*) and adverbs (*slowly*), but before nouns (*details, information*).

● Note that we use *too many/too few* with countable nouns and *too much/too little* with uncountable nouns.

● To show a result, *too* and *not enough* can be followed by *to* + infinitive, or *for* + someone, or both.

*The price is **too** high **to accept** your proposal.*
*The price is **too** high **for** us.*
*The price is **too** high **for** us **to accept** your proposal.*

B So/such

● We use *so* and *such (a)* for emphasis.

adjectives	*She is **so good** at giving presentations.*
adverbs	*She gives presentations **so well**.*
nouns: countable	*There were **so many diagrams** in the report.*
	*She gave **such a good presentation**.*
	*She gives **such good presentations**.*
nouns: uncountable	*There was **so much information** in the report.*
	*She gave me **such good advice**.* (NOT ~~such a good advice~~)

● Note that we use *so many/so few* with countable nouns and *so much/so little* with uncountable nouns.

C So/too

● *So* and *too* are different. *Too* suggests that something cannot be done or something will not happen. Compare:

It's so expensive. (it's very expensive, but maybe I will buy it anyway)
It's too expensive. (it's very expensive, and because of that I will not buy it)

Exercises

51.1 Complete the sentences with either *too* or *enough*. Leave one gap empty each time.

1 It's not a good job – the salary is _____*too*_____ low _____
2 It's not a good job – the salary isn't _____ high _____
3 This report is full of mistakes – you've checked it _____ quickly _____
4 This report is full of mistakes – you haven't checked it _____ carefully _____
5 The project is running late – there isn't _____ time _____ to finish everything.
6 The project is running late – there's been _____ much wasted time _____
7 They'll have to cut some jobs – there are _____ many employees _____
8 They'll have to recruit more people – there aren't _____ employees _____

51.2 Complete the sentences with either *so* or *such* or *such a*.

1 That's _____ good idea – let's put it on the agenda for the next meeting.
2 That idea is _____ good – let's put it on the agenda for the next meeting.
3 You always have _____ good ideas – it's great to have you on the team.
4 We have a new website – it's _____ easy to find what you want now.
5 We have a new website – it has _____ amazing graphics.
6 We have a new website – it's made _____ difference to the business.

51.3 <u>Underline</u> the correct words.

1 I had *so many/so much* reports to finish that I stayed in the office until nine.
2 He's earning *so many/so much* money that he bought a second yacht.
3 I need a bigger office – there's *so few/so little* space for all my stuff.
4 I rarely watch TV – there are *so few/so little* good programmes.
5 We're going bankrupt. It's *so late/too late* to rescue the company.
6 The new model was launched *so late/too late*. But it sold very well in the end.

58 **51.4** Complete the text with these words: *so, such a, so much, so many, too many, not enough*.

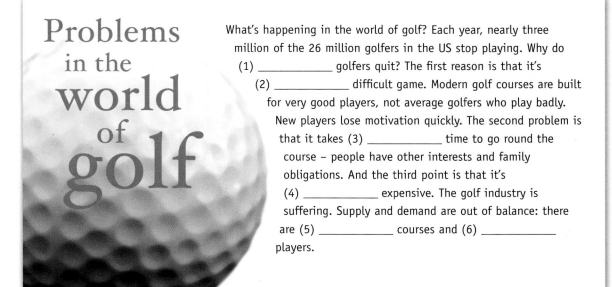

Problems in the world of golf

What's happening in the world of golf? Each year, nearly three million of the 26 million golfers in the US stop playing. Why do (1) _____ golfers quit? The first reason is that it's (2) _____ difficult game. Modern golf courses are built for very good players, not average golfers who play badly. New players lose motivation quickly. The second problem is that it takes (3) _____ time to go round the course – people have other interests and family obligations. And the third point is that it's (4) _____ expensive. The golf industry is suffering. Supply and demand are out of balance: there are (5) _____ courses and (6) _____ players.

52 Linking words 1

A Addition: *both ... and .../as well as*

● We can emphasize the fact that there are two things. Note the positions.

*J.P. Morgan are involved in **both** investment **and** retail banking.*
*J.P. Morgan are involved in investment banking **and also** retail banking.*
*J.P. Morgan are involved in investment banking **and** retail banking **too/as well**.*
*J.P. Morgan are involved in investment banking **as well as** retail banking.*

B Contrast: *but/although/(even) though*

● *But* introduces a contrast, and this can be different or surprising.

*The traffic was terrible yesterday, **but** it's better today.* (different)
*The traffic was terrible, **but** I arrived on time.* (surprising)

● A clause with *although* makes the information in the other clause seem surprising or interesting.

*I arrived on time **although** the traffic was terrible.* ('arriving on time' is surprising)

Although can come at the beginning of the sentence.

***Although** the traffic was terrible, I arrived on time.*

● We can use *though* and *even though* like *although*. *Though* is used in informal speech and writing. *Even though* makes a strong contrast.

*I don't agree with her, **though** I can see what she's saying.*
*The European Union is stable and successful, **even though** some of its members were at war with each other in the last century.*

C Contrast: *despite/in spite of*

● *Despite* and *in spite of* are followed by a noun or noun phrase.

***Despite my cold**, I went to work.* (NOT subject + verb: ~~Despite I had a cold~~)

● The *-ing* form of the verb can act like a noun.

***Despite having a cold**, I went to work.*

D Reason and result: *because/so*

● We use *because* when we want to explain the reason for something.

*We're going to change our supplier **because** we get so many incorrect orders.*

● *As* and *since* are similar to *because*. They are common at the beginning of the sentence. *Since* is a little more formal.

***Since** we have had so many incorrect orders and late deliveries, we are writing to inform you that we will no longer be using your services.*

● We use *so* to express a result. Compare *because* and *so*:

*We're going to change our supplier **because** we get so many incorrect orders.*
*We get so many incorrect orders, **so** we're going to change our supplier.*

CBarsotti

"No, Hoskins, you're not going to do it just because I'm telling you to do it. You're going to do it because you believe in it."

Exercises

52.1 <u>Underline</u> the one correct word in each sentence.

  1 We sell women's clothing and accessories *both/<u>too</u>/as well as*.

  2 We sell women's clothing *also/as well/as well as* accessories.

  3 *Although/Despite/But* the traffic, I managed to get here just in time.

  4 It was a useful meeting, *despite/although/so* I'm pleased I went.

  5 It was a useful meeting, *despite/although/so* all the disagreements.

  6 It was a useful meeting, *despite/although/so* there were a lot of disagreements.

  7 We saw a fall in sales *in spite of/because/so* our competitors dropped their prices.

  8 Our competitors dropped their prices *in spite of/because/so* we saw a fall in sales.

  9 We saw a fall in sales, *in spite of/because/so* launching several new products.

 10 *As/So/Also* you have not contacted us, we are asking our lawyers to take action.

52.2 Choose the best linking word and join the sentences.

  1 We offer good quality. We offer cheap prices. (although/as well as/because)
     We offer good quality as well as cheap prices.

  2 My English is quite good. I lived in London for two years. (despite/also/because)

     _____

  3 I lived in London for two years. My English is quite good. (despite/also/so)

     _____

  4 I like my job. It's not well-paid. (also/even though/because)

     _____

  5 It was getting late. I decided to go home. (so/despite/too)

     _____

  6 It was getting late. I decided to go home. (as/despite/too)

     _____

52.3 Complete this email with these words: *as, ~~as well~~, even though, in spite of, so.*

● ● ●
Subject   fruit products from the Ukraine
I represent a company working in the food sector in the Ukraine – our main product is fruit jam, but we produce canned fruit (1) _____*as well*_____ . We have had some success exporting to European countries, (2) _____ Ukraine is not a member of the EU. I am writing this email (3) _____ I think there may be a good business opportunity for both of us. Your company owns a chain of independent supermarkets in Germany, (4) _____ you must be interested in finding new suppliers such as ourselves. (5) _____ our very competitive prices, our jams are high quality, and made with organically grown fruit. If you would like to discuss this matter further, please email me or call me on my direct line. The details are below.

 **Linking words 2**

A Words meaning *and*, *but* and *so*

- *And*, *but* and *so* join parts of the same sentence. We can use longer words and phrases to link across different sentences or paragraphs.

  and   *in addition, as well as this, besides this, moreover* (formal)
  but   *however, on the other hand, nevertheless* (formal)
  so   *therefore, as a result, consequently* (formal)

  Most people will receive a pension from the state when they retire. **In addition**, *some people may get money from a company pension scheme.* **However**, *this may not be enough to provide for a comfortable old age.* **Therefore**, *you should consider saving money in a private pension plan as well.*

B For example/for instance/such as

- To give examples we can use *for example* or *for instance*. Note the positions.

  Some countries have unusual food. **For example** *in Sweden fruit soup is common.*
  Some countries have unusual food. In Sweden, **for example**, *fruit soup is common.*

- We can use *such as* in the middle of a sentence to give examples.

  In East Asian countries, **such as** *China and Japan, people save a higher proportion of their income than in the US or Europe.*

C In fact/actually/as a matter of fact

- We use *in fact, actually, as a matter of fact* to say what is really true, when this is surprising or different to what people think.

  Many people have the stereotype that in Latin countries people arrive late for meetings. **In fact**, *in the modern business world this is not true.*

- Note that *actually* does not mean *now/currently*. This is a common mistake.

D Firstly/finally

- We can use *first, firstly* and *first of all* to begin a list of points. For other points we use *second, secondly, third, thirdly,* etc. To finish the sequence we say *finally*.

E To summarise/basically

- To finish by summarising or saying the most important point we can use:
  to summarise, in short, basically, taking everything into consideration.

  The Internet has changed the way that people shop. **First of all**, *it's much easier to compare prices.* **Secondly**, *it's more convenient because you don't have to walk from store to store.* **Finally**, *it's easier to find specialist products.* **Basically**, *any retailer that doesn't have a strong online presence will probably go out of business.*

Exercises

53.1 Complete each sentence with a pair of words. Choose from: *for instance/in addition, however/therefore, in fact/basically, ~~secondly/however~~.*

1 If you are ill and cannot come to work, there is a procedure to follow. Firstly, you should call the office before 9am. _____*Secondly*_____ , you need to get a doctor's note. _____*However*_____ , if you are ill for only one or two days, you do not need a note.

2 We've made many improvements to our brochure this year. _____ , the quality of the photographs is better, the technical specifications are easier to understand, and there is a clear index. _____ , for the first time we will include a list of key sales staff and their email addresses.

3 There is some flexibility in the negotiations at this stage. _____ , when you sign the contract it becomes legally binding. _____ , we strongly recommend that you review it with a lawyer first.

4 Our Marketing Director has just left the company. _____ , he's going to work for our main competitor. Also, our new range of products won't be on the shelves until after Christmas. _____ , things aren't looking too good right now.

53.2 Tick (✓) the four sentences that are possible. Cross (✗) the two that are not.

1 Actually, we thought we'd finish at five not six.

2 We thought we'd finish actually at five not six.

3 We thought we'd finish at five actually, not six.

4 We thought we'd finish at five, but we actually finished at six.

5 We thought we'd finish at five, but actually we finished at six.

6 We thought we'd finish at five, but we finished at actually six.

53.3 Complete this article about alternative investments by choosing the right words.

Contemporary art: a good investment?

These days investors want to spread their risk and diversify into new asset classes. (1) *As a result/On the other hand*, there is growing demand for high-quality contemporary art. Do you think it's too risky? (2) *Besides this/Actually*, it's not. The Mei/Moses All Art Index shows that over the last fifty years the art market has performed slightly better than the equity market. So it's a good investment for the long term. (3) *As a result/Besides this* there's another advantage: owning art gives you status and is good for your image. (4) *On the other hand/Taking everything into consideration* there are disadvantages to having a Picasso in your house. Have you thought about the security you're going to need? And what happens if your chosen artist goes out of fashion? (5) *On the other hand/Taking everything into consideration*, buying art as an investment deserves serious consideration. It's a great way to diversify your portfolio, but it's probably only for wealthy investors.

A Purpose: *to/for/so that*

- To give the reason for doing something (purpose) we can use *to*, *for* or *so that*. They are followed by different structures. Study the table and notes below.

to/in order to + infinitive	*I'm calling **to ask** about our last order.* (NOT ~~for ask~~ or ~~for to ask~~) *I went **to see** what the problem was.* (NOT ~~for see~~ or ~~for to see~~)
for + noun or pronoun	*I went to London **for an interview**.* *She did it **for love**, not **for money**.*
for + -ing	*This machine is **for cutting** and **shaping** the metal.* (used to say why we use a piece of equipment or software)
so that + subject + verb	*I'll call you tomorrow **so (that) I can** discuss the contract in more detail.* *I'll reconfirm the return flight **so (that) there's** no problem.*

- In the first row above, *in order to* is more formal than *to*.

  *I am giving this press conference **in order to clarify** our financial situation.*

- If the subject of both clauses is the same, we can use *to* or *so that*.

  <u>The auditors</u> are coming **to check**/**so that** <u>they</u> **can check** our accounts.

  But if the two subjects are different, we can only use *so that*.

  <u>The auditors</u> are coming **so that** <u>I</u> **can ask** them some questions.

B *Like/as/as if*

- We can use *like* or *as* to mean 'in the way that'. *Like* is more common.

  *Leave everything just **like**/**as** you found it.*
  *No-one can play the trumpet **like**/**as** Miles Davis could.*

- Before a noun or pronoun (where there is no subject + verb) we must use *like*.

  *You look **like your brother**.* (NOT ~~as your brother~~)
  *This supplier, **like all the others**, is very unreliable.* (NOT ~~as all the others~~)

- We use *like* to give examples.

  *Some countries, **like** Sweden, have strong environmental policies.* (NOT ~~as Sweden~~)

- We use *as* to say what job/function/role a person or thing has.

  *She works **as a consultant**.* (NOT ~~like a consultant~~)
  *We use this room **as a storage area**.* (NOT ~~like a storage area~~)

- To say something is probable we can use *it looks* with *like* or *as if*.

  *It looks **like** our new range will be in the shops next week.*
  *It looks **as if** our new range will be in the shops next week.*

"As your attorney, Roger, I feel it's my duty to charge you an enormous amount of money."

Exercises

54.1 <u>Underline</u> the correct words.

1   We delayed the advertising campaign *to/<u>for</u>* a very good reason.

2   I became a freelancer *to have/for to have* more control over my life.

3   I downloaded a program *for telephone/for telephoning* over the Internet.

4   *In order to/For* write my report, I need to collect some more information.

5   We'll stop the meeting *so/to* everyone can have a short break.

6   We'll stop the meeting *so/to* have a short break.

7   We'll stop the meeting *so/for* a short break.

8   We have to improve quality *so that/to* we can compete with Asia.

9   We have to improve quality *so that/to* compete with Asia.

10   Our sales staff use a hand-held computer *to recording/for recording* customer details.

54.2 Complete each sentence with: *to, for, so that.*

1   I'm here today _____*to*_____ tell you about our wonderful new cleaning product.

2   I'm here today _____ I can tell you about our wonderful new cleaning product.

3   I'm here today _____ the sales conference.

4   We need profits _____ our shareholders are happy.

5   We need profits _____ our reinvestment program.

6   We need profits _____ stay in business, of course.

54.3 <u>Underline</u> the six correct words from the total of eight in *italics*.

1   We'll send out a mailing, *like/as* we did before.

2   I'm going to buy a laptop *like/as* yours.

3   It looks *like/as if* it's going to rain.

4   She works *like/as* a financial analyst.

54.4 Complete this article using these words: *as, for, like, so that, to.*

Fake goods: be careful what you buy

A woman phoned Pfizer on its customer hotline (1) _____ complain about the strange taste of a cholesterol-lowering drug she was taking. Pfizer asked her to send the bottle of pills (2) _____ analysis. They discovered that the pills were fakes (counterfeits), even though they looked (3) _____ the real thing. This is not an isolated case. Producers of counterfeit goods copy well-known brands in all sectors: consumer electronics, luxury goods, auto parts, and more. They take the risk (4) _____ they can make a profit. And the problem is huge and growing. In fact, the World Customs Organization estimates that 7% of world trade now involves fake goods. It looks (5) _____ if this is one issue that just won't go away.

55 Verb + preposition

A Introduction

● Here is a list of verbs and the prepositions that normally follow them.

apply for	*decide on*	*listen to*
ask for	*depend on*	*pay for*
believe in	*focus on*	*rely on*
belong to	*happen to*	*specialize in*
benefit from	*hope for*	*suffer from*
compete against	*insist on*	*sympathize with*
consist of	*know about*	*take care of*
co-operate with	*lead to*	*wait for*

● In *wh-* questions the preposition usually goes at the end.

*What job are you applying **for**?* (NOT ~~For what job are you applying~~?)
*What does it depend **on**?* (NOT ~~On what does it depend~~?)
*Who are you waiting **for**?* (NOT ~~For who are you waiting~~?)

B Verb + different prepositions

● Some verbs are followed by one preposition for a thing, and another for a person.

agree to (thing)	*complain about* (thing)	*talk about* (thing)
agree with (person)	*complain to* (person)	*talk to* (person)
apologize for (thing)	*hear about* (thing)	*write about* (thing)
apologize to (person)	*hear from* (person)	*write to* (person)

*They **agreed to** a discount of 3%./They **agreed with** me.*
*I **apologize for** my poor handwriting./I got very angry – I must **apologize to** her.*
*Have you **heard about** the merger?/Have you **heard from** Frankie recently?*

C Verb + object + preposition

● Some verbs are followed by an object (thing or person) before the preposition.

ask person *for*	*insure* thing *against*	*spend* thing *on*
blame person *for*	*invest* thing *in*	*split* thing *into*
borrow thing *from*	*invite* person *to*	*supply* person *with*
congratulate person *on*	*protect* person *from*	*thank* person *for*
divide thing *into*	*provide* person *with*	*translate* thing *into*

D Verb + no preposition

● The verbs *call, phone, tell, discuss* are not usually followed by a preposition.

I called my boss. (NOT ~~called to~~)
We discussed the project. (NOT ~~discussed about~~)

Exercises

55.1 <u>Underline</u> the correct preposition.

1 Something very funny happened <u>to</u>/with/for me yesterday.
2 Our success depends of/from/on the relationship we have with our customers.
3 I do a lot of charity work in my free time – I belong in/to/with the Rotary Club.
4 I sympathize for/with/to your problem, but there's very little I can do.
5 At the meeting we'll have to decide on/in/for what to do next.
6 The boss wants to see me for a moment – can you take care from/on/of this customer?
7 Please, let me pay the bill. I insist for/on/in it.
8 The Faculty of Business and Management consists with/in/of five departments.
9 There is no doubt that stress can lead on/for/to physical illness.
10 Can we rely on/from/of him to support us in the meeting?

55.2 Complete each sentence with one of these verbs: *agree, ~~apologize~~, hear*
and one of these prepositions: *about, from, for, ~~to~~, to, with*.

1 I need to ____apologize____ _____to_____ Jackie for what I said to her in the bar last night.
2 I must _____ _____ not contacting you sooner, but I've been very busy.
3 I _____ _____ you in principle, but I'm not sure about the details.
4 We _____ _____ your price, on condition that you accept our quality standards.
5 Thank you for your email, and I hope to _____ _____ you soon.
6 Have you _____ _____ the reorganization plans?

55.3 Tick (✓) two sentences that are already correct. Add the word *to*, in the right place, to two sentences.

1 Who does this belong?
2 I phoned Flavia this morning.
3 I told the printers about the artwork.
4 What is this going to lead?

55.4 Complete this email with these prepositions: *against, for, for, in, on, with*.

● ● ●
Subject   health and safety insurance

Erik – we've invested a lot of money (1) _____ the new factory, but we haven't spent any money (2) _____ insurance cover. What happens if there's an industrial accident and the person concerned blames us (3) _____ any injuries they receive? We need to insure ourselves (4) _____ claims of this nature. Injured workers will ask us (5) _____ compensation, and we might have to provide them (6) _____ hospital expenses as well as a salary while they are not working.

A Introduction

● Here is a list of adjectives and the prepositions that can follow them:

accustomed to	fed up with	relevant to
afraid of	full of	rich in
attached to	guilty of	right about
aware of	important for	safe from
bored with	interested in	satisfied with
certain about	involved in	serious about
compatible with	late for	similar to
covered in	married to	suitable for
dependent on	opposed to	surprised at/by
different from/to	pleased with	suspicious of
disappointed by/about	popular with	typical of
doubtful about	prepared for	used to (= accustomed to)
enthusiastic about	proud of	useful for
famous for	ready for	worried about
fascinated by	related to	wrong about

"Thank you, sir. I am proud of my resume. And I think you'll find that most of it is true."

● For behaviour towards another person we use adjective + *to*. Examples include: *good to, kind to, nice to, polite to, rude to.*

It's a golden rule: never be **rude to** *your customers.*

● When a preposition is followed by a verb, the -*ing* form must be used.

Are you **serious about outsourcing** *our back-office functions to India?*

B Adjective + choice of preposition

● Some adjectives are followed by one preposition for a thing, and another for a person.

angry about (thing)	*good/bad at* (doing something)	*sorry about* (thing)
angry with (person)	*good/bad for* (thing)	*sorry for* (doing something)
annoyed about (thing)	*responsible for* (thing)	*(feel) sorry for* (person)
annoyed with (person)	*responsible to* (person)	

I'm **annoyed about** *the strike – it's really going to disrupt our production.*
I'm **annoyed with** *myself for making such a silly mistake.*
Jack is **good at** *coaching new employees.*
Low interest rates are **good for** *business.*
I'm **responsible for** *sales and marketing in Spain.*
I'm **responsible to** *the Marketing Director, Mrs Carvalho.*
I'm **sorry about** *what happened yesterday.*
I'm **sorry for** *being late.*
I feel **sorry for** *David – he lost his job because of a reorganization in the company.*

Exercises

56.1 Complete sentences 1–8 with endings a)–h).

1	Our company is famous	a)	with Windows?
2	Is this software compatible	b)	about this, but I think it's a waste of money.
3	She was full	c)	for the quality of its engineering.
4	I could be wrong	d)	in any other items from the catalogue?
5	I was surprised	e)	of enthusiasm when I explained our idea.
6	Are you interested	f)	to delays on the metro. They're very common.
7	We're used	g)	from the old one in several important ways.
8	This model is different	h)	by the changes in Indonesia since my last visit.

56.2 Complete each sentence with an adjective: *attached, aware, rich, safe, ~~suitable~~*
and a preposition: *~~for~~, from, of, in, to.*

1 This fund is _____*suitable*_____ _____*for*_____ investors prepared to accept a high level of risk.
2 Russia is very _____ _____ natural resources.
3 There is a copy of the contract _____ _____ this letter.
4 The firewall should make your network _____ _____ hackers and viruses.
5 I don't think he's _____ _____ the difficulties he's creating.

56.3 <u>Underline</u> the correct word.

1 I'm very angry *about/with* them for causing this delay.
2 I'm very angry *about/with* the delay.
3 A new person at the top would be good *at/for* the company.
4 A Human Resources manager has to be good *at/for* dealing with conflict.
5 I'm responsible *for/to* all the transport and logistics.
6 The Finance Director is directly responsible *for/to* the CEO.

56.4 Complete part of a telephone conversation using: *about, by, for, ~~in~~, of, on, to, with.*

HANS: I'm interested (1) _____*in*_____ using your hotel for our next conference, and I'd like to ask one or two questions to check that it is suitable (2) _____ our requirements.

KIRSTEN: Yes, of course. Our hotel is very popular (3) _____ conference organizers, and we are used (4) _____ handling all the necessary arrangements.

HANS: Good. The first thing is numbers. I'm not certain (5) _____ this, but there could be over a hundred delegates. Last year we were surprised (6) _____ the number of people.

KIRSTEN: That number of people is typical (7) _____ the conferences we have here and it shouldn't be a problem. However it is dependent to some extent (8) _____ the time of year. We're already very busy over the summer period and we may not be able to accommodate you at that time.

*Outsourcing of infotech and business processing work could be going **out of favour**, according to two studies that suggest big companies are rethinking the concept and bringing operations back in-house.*

The BusinessTimes website

Here is a list of common prepositional phrases (preposition + noun phrase).

at	*at first sight, at a good price, at a profit/loss, at short notice*
	*We sold the business **at a good price/at a loss/at a profit**.*
by	*by accident, by car/taxi/bus, by chance, by credit card, by email, by hand, by law, by mistake*
	*It wasn't planned – it just happened **by accident/by chance/by mistake**.*
for	*for a change, for lunch, for rent, for sale*
	*They are redeveloping this area and soon there will be a lot of apartments **for sale/for rent**.*
in	*in advance, in cash, in debt, in the end, in-house, in a hurry, in the market* (companies)*, in person, in stock, in time* (= early enough to do something)*, in touch, in trouble, in writing*
	*You have to pay 20% of the total cost **in advance**.*
	*Our company has been **in debt/in the market/in trouble** for a long time.*
	*It was great seeing you again! Have a good flight and keep **in touch**.*
	*I'll let you know **in advance/in person/in time/in writing**.*
on	*on budget, on business, on demand, on foot, on hold, on holiday, on the Internet, online, on the market* (products)*, on order, on the other line, on purpose, on sale, on schedule, on strike, on target, on time* (= at the right time)*, on track, on vacation*
	*I found some information about their company **on the Internet/online**.*
	*This product has been **on the market/on sale** for over a year.*
	*Don't worry, we'll get to the airport **on time**.*
	*Things are going as planned – we're **on track** to increase sales by 20% this year.*
	*I'm sorry, but she's not available. She's **on holiday/on the other line/on vacation**.*
out of	*out of date, out of favour, out of order, out of stock*
	*Our software is **out of date** – there's a much better version available now.*
under	*under pressure*
	*We're really **under pressure** to meet all our deadlines.*
up to	*up to date, up to you*
	*Our software is completely **up to date** – I've just installed the latest version.*
	*You can pay now or later – it's **up to you**.*

"I'm not looking forward to telling the 300 salesmen we're going to start selling on the Internet."

Exercises

57.1 <u>Underline</u> the correct prepositions.

1 Because of the emergency, I had to arrange this meeting *with/at* short notice.

2 Did you come *in/by* car or *on/with* foot?

3 'Can I pay *by/in* credit card?' – 'Of course, or *for/in* cash if you prefer'.

4 *By/At* first sight it looks like a good idea, but I need to see all the details *on/in* writing.

5 *By/On* law the trade union is not allowed to go *by/on* strike unless it holds a ballot of all the members.

6 I'm sorry, the colour you want is *under/out of* stock. It should be *up/in* stock again next week.

7 I'm sorry, Mr Cutting is *on/in* the other line at the moment. If you're *in/under* a hurry I can take a message and ask him to call you back.

8 We should arrive at the airport *on/by* time, but I don't think we'll be *on/in* time to do any shopping.

57.2 One phrase in each group does not match. Cross it out.

1	to sell something …	at a good price, at a profit, ~~in trouble~~, on the Internet
2	to arrive …	by taxi, on order, on foot, in time
3	to pay …	on time, by credit card, in advance, out of stock
4	to be …	in debt, in the end, for sale, in stock
5	to be …	by hand, out of stock, under pressure, out of date
6	to do something …	by mistake, in a hurry, up to you, on purpose
7	to offer a service …	on demand, on business, online, at a good price
8	to meet someone …	by chance, in writing, in person, for lunch
9	to finish a project …	on order, on time, on budget, on schedule
10	to keep a project …	on target, on track, on hold, on business

62

57.3 Complete this advertisement using these prepositions: *at, at, by, ~~in~~, on, on, on, on, under, up*.

(IT) Solutions

We understand all your information technology needs.

○ Do you need to upgrade your hardware
(1) _____*in*_____ a hurry?

○ We can supply you (2) _____ time and
(3) _____ a good price.

○ Are you (4) _____ pressure because of
a software problem? Don't worry – we'll fix it
(5) _____ short notice.

○ Do you have an IT project you need to keep
(6) _____ track? We'll work with you to
make sure that the project runs (7) _____
budget and (8) _____ schedule.

○ To find out more information, just contact
us (9) _____ email. Now it's
(10) _____ to you!

"It's up to you now, Miller. The only thing that can save us is an accounting breakthrough."

58 Prepositions of place

A At/in/on

- *At* is used to show the place or position of someone or something.

  *I'll meet you **at** the main entrance.*   *Does this train stop **at** Lille?*
  *I was waiting **at** the bus stop.*   *Why isn't he **at** his desk?*

- *In* means inside a container, place or area.

  *Her passport was **in** her bag.*   *Our clothes are manufactured **in** Turkey.*

  In is also used to show movement or looking into a place.

  *The door was open so I walked **in**.*   *Look **in** the top drawer of my desk.*

- *On* means touching the surface of something.

  *I have a picture of my wife and children **on** my desk.*   (horizontal surface)
  *There's a clock **on** the wall over there.*   (vertical surface)
  *In Portugal you kiss a woman **on** the cheek three times.*

B Expressions with *at/in/on*

- Here are some fixed expressions with *at*.

***at** the front/back*	***at** the top/bottom*	***at** the beginning/end*
***at** the station/airport*	***at** home/work* (NOT ~~at the home, at the work~~)	

- Here are some fixed expressions with *in*.

***in** the middle*	***in** the corner*	***in** a book/magazine/newspaper*
***in** the photo/picture*	***in** line/a queue*	***in** hospital* (NOT ~~in the hospital~~)
***in** the chair* (= in charge of the meeting)		***in** the country* (= in a rural area)

- Here are some fixed expressions with *on*.

***on** the left/right*	***on** the first floor*	***on** the platform/pavement*
***on** page 24*	***on** the page/map*	***on** the phone/the computer*
***on** the screen*	***on** the plane/bus/train* (BUT ***in** a car/taxi*)	

C Above/below and over/under

- *Above/below* mean 'higher' and 'lower'. They are used to talk about positions, amounts and locations in documents.

  *The accounts department is on the floor **above/below** this one.*
  *Sales are **below average** for this time of year.*
  *Operating profit increased in all markets – see the table **below** for more details.*

- *Over/under* are very similar to *above/below*. Use *over/under* for amount, movement, and when one thing covers another.

  *The material costs **over/under** €15 a metre.*
  *The plane flew **over** the Alps.*
  *We sailed **under** the bridge.*
  *I put my hands **over** my ears.* (covering)
  *I sat **under** the tree.* (covered by)

Exercises

58.1 Complete the sentences with *at* (x2), *in* (x2) or *on* (x2).

1 Germany has the biggest economy _____ Europe.

2 I'll meet you _____ the statue in the main square in twenty minutes.

3 There's some more paper for the photocopier _____ the shelf.

4 I put my hand _____ my pocket but my wallet had gone.

5 Never touch a Thai person _____ the head – it's a social taboo.

6 Waiter, can we sit _____ the table over there by the window?

58.2 Complete the sentences with *at, in* or *on*.

1 He'll be with you in a moment – he's just __on__ the phone.

2 At the next meeting Sandra is going to be _____ the chair.

3 I often work _____ home in the evenings.

4 When I retire I'd like to live _____ the country.

5 It's a large office block, and our offices are _____ the seventh floor.

6 Hungary has an excellent location right _____ the middle of Europe.

7 The figures appear in the Appendix _____ the back of the report.

8 Go down Church Street and you'll see our offices _____ the right.

9 Can you increase the size of the text _____ the screen?

10 I was standing _____ line for twenty minutes at the security checkpoint.

58.3 Complete the sentences by using these words once each: *above, below, over, under.*

1 I crossed _____ to the other side of the street.

2 This issue has already been discussed in section 2.4.1 _____ .

3 It was really cold – I'm sure the temperature was _____ zero.

4 The memo you wrote is somewhere _____ that pile of reports.

58.4 Complete this email with *at, in* or *on*.

Subject   artwork for brochure

Celia – just a few comments on the artwork you sent me:

1 The front cover looks great. But I think that the company logo should be (1) _____ the top of the page, not (2) _____ the middle where it is now.

2 The text and the photograph (3) _____ page six need to be closer together. Perhaps the photograph could be (4) _____ the corner, (5) _____ the right? Also, the text itself is quite long – couldn't we cut a paragraph (6) _____ the end?

I hope that's clear. If you need to contact me, you can call me (7) _____ home this evening, or try calling me (8) _____ my cell phone.

A What is a phrasal verb?

- A phrasal verb is a combination of a verb (*put*, *take*) and a preposition (*back*, *off*). The meaning comes from the combination of the two words. Compare:

Phrasal verb	**Verb + preposition**
*The deal **fell through**.*	*He **fell through** the air on a parachute.*
(*fall* + *through* = fail to happen)	(*fall* and *through* both have their normal, separate meanings)
*I **looked up** his name in the telephone directory.*	*I **looked up** at the sky.*
(*look* + *up* = find in a list)	(*look* and *up* both have their normal, separate meanings)

The examples on the left are phrasal verbs. The examples on the right are not.

- Sometimes a phrasal verb has the same meaning as a one-word verb. The phrasal verb is usually more informal.

   cut back = reduce   *find out* = discover   *go back* = return

- Sometimes we have to use the phrasal verb: there is no one-word verb.

   *I **look forward to** meeting you.*   *The plane **took off**.*   *I **got up** at six this morning.*

IT'S A 300 PAGE GOVERNMENT QUESTIONNAIRE ABOUT CUTTING BACK ON BUREAUCRACY!

B Separable phrasal verbs

*Our coaches will **pick you up** within 10 minutes and take you from the car park to the airport terminal.*

Parking Express website

- With some phrasal verbs we can separate the two parts.
- When the object is a noun, we can put it in two places.

   *Can you pick **Patricia** up from the station?*
   *Can you pick up **Patricia** from the station?*

- When the object is a pronoun, it must come in the middle.

   *Can you pick **me** up from the station?* (NOT ~~pick up me~~)

- When the object is a long phrase, it must come after the phrasal verb.

   *Can you pick up **the Chinese visitors who are arriving tomorrow** from the station?*

C List of separable phrasal verbs

*American Airlines will **lay off** 3100 flight attendants beginning July 1 -- a result of cost-cutting moves and recent talks with the flight attendants' union.*

CNN website

- The meanings below are approximate. Check in a dictionary.

back up = make a copy on a computer	*keep down* = prevent from increasing
back up = give support to	*lay off* = dismiss, stop employing
check out = find more information about	*look up* = find in a book or a list
close down = stop operating as a business	*pick up* = collect in a car
cut back = reduce	*put off* = delay
cut off = disconnect	*ring/call up* = telephone someone
draw up = prepare and write	*set up* = start a business
drop off = take to a place in a car	*sort out* = organize, deal with, find a solution
figure out = understand, find an answer to	*take over* = get control of another company
fill in = add information in a document	*throw away* = dispose of, get rid of
find out = discover a fact	*turn down* = refuse, say 'no' to
hold up = cause a delay	*turn on/off* = start/stop a piece of equipment

Exercises

59.1 Cross out the one option each time that is not correct.

1   I *set the business up/set it up/set up the business/~~set up it~~* in 2004.

2   You must *fill in the form/fill the form in/fill in it/fill it in*.

3   Please *turn the computer off/turn off the computer/turn off it/turn it off*.

4   Can you *pick me up/pick up me/pick Mr Chavez up/pick up Mr Chavez*?

59.2 Match the beginnings and endings of the sentences.

1   You can drop off   ☐   a)   if you're using a cell phone in a railway tunnel.

2   You can sort out   ☐   b)   your children at school on the way to work.

3   You can lay off   ☐   c)   somebody in a meeting if you agree with them.

4   You can back up   ☐   d)   the mess in your office.

5   You can be cut off ☐   e)   the chance to do a language course in the UK.

6   Don't turn down   ☐   f)   workers if demand for your products goes down.

59.3 <u>Underline</u> the correct word.

1   We don't have an office in Birmingham any more. Unfortunately, we had to *keep/close/turn/lay* it down.

2   Friday afternoon is not a good time to have the meeting – everyone is out of the office. Let's *turn/cut/drop/put* it off until Monday.

3   The result of the negotiation has been good for both sides. Now our lawyers will *draw/hold/back/sort* up a contract, and we'll send it to you by the end of the month.

4   We don't have a presence in their market at the moment. The best option is probably to *find/set/take/pick* over a local company with a strong position.

59.4 Complete this telephone dialogue by choosing the correct word in brackets.

BRUCE: Jiao, I've got a problem here – can you help me to sort it (1) _____ (up/out/over)?
The customs office in Guangzhou is holding (2) _____ (up/off/down) a shipment of the goods we need. I think there's an issue with the paperwork.

JIAO: OK, I can call the Guangzhou customs office and try to find (3) _____ (away/up/out) what the problem is.

BRUCE: Thanks, I'd appreciate that. All the documents have been scanned and backed (4) _____ (over/up/over) at this end, and I can send copies as an email attachment.

JIAO: That's good. If necessary I can go to the customs office in person and drop (5) _____ (off/out/down) anything they need.

A Introduction

● Some phrasal verbs are 'inseparable': the parts cannot be separated.

call for = collect someone from a place	*get back to* = contact at a later time
call on = visit for a short time	*get over* = recover from a bad experience
come across = find by chance	*go through* = examine carefully
deal with = take action in relation to	*look after* = take care of
deal with = do business with	*look forward to* = feel happy about a future event
deal with = be about a subject	*look into* = investigate, examine the facts
do without = succeed in working without	*look through* = search among a lot of things
face up to = deal with something difficult	*take up* = fill an amount of time

*In my job I **deal with** customer services.* (NOT ~~deal customer services with~~)
*I **look forward to** your visit.* (NOT ~~look your visit forward to~~)

B Phrasal verbs with no object

● Some phrasal verbs do not take an object. They are 'intransitive'.

break down = stop working	*get along/on* = make progress
check in = arrive and give your details	*grow up* = change from child to adult
come down = become less in amount	*hold/hang on* = wait
fall through = fail to happen	*take off* = leave the ground and start to fly

The photocopier has broken down. (NOT ~~Someone has broken down the photocopier.~~)
I grew up in Lyon. (NOT ~~I grew up my family in Lyon.~~)

C Phrasal verb + preposition + object

● Many phrasal verbs can be used either with no object, or followed by a preposition + object.

carry on (with) = continue doing	*get on (with)* = continue after an interruption
catch up (with) = reach the same point as	*get through (to)* = succeed in reaching by phone
cut down (on) = reduce, do less of	*join in (with)* = take part in an activity
drop in (on) = visit for a short time	*keep up (with)* = know about what is happening
fit in (with) = exist together easily	*move on (to)* = start doing something new
get along/on (with) = be friendly with	*run out (of)* = finish your supply of something

These examples show the verbs without and with an object.

*It's a good place to work. We all **get along** really well.*
*It's a good place to work. We all **get along with each other** really well.*
*Any more comments? OK, shall we **move on**?*
*Any more comments? OK, shall we **move on to the next item** on the agenda?*

Exercises

60.1 Read 1–3, then match the uses of *deal with* to the definitions a)–c) below.

1　I've spent all morning *dealing with* a problem on the network.　☐
2　This report *deals with* the company's long-term strategy.　☐
3　We've been *dealing with* this particular supplier for many years.　☐

　　a) do business with　　　b) take action in relation to　　　c) be about a subject

60.2 Match the beginnings and endings of the sentences.

1　I'm looking after　☐　　a)　meeting you in Paris next month.
2　I'm looking forward to　☐　　b)　the cause of the fire.
3　I'm looking into　☐　　c)　my records to see if I can find his name.
4　I'm looking through　☐　　d)　the office while Eva is on her lunch-break.

60.3 Rewrite each sentence so that it contains the word in brackets.

1　The lift has stopped working. (break) _The lift has broken down._
2　How are you making progress? (get) _____
3　The negotiations have failed. (fall) _____
4　Inflation is becoming less. (come) _____
5　Wait for a moment while I find a pen. (hold) _____

60.4 Complete the sentences with one word from list A and one word from list B.

A: down　in　~~on~~　out　through　　　B: of　on　to　~~with~~　with

1　Has everyone finished their coffee? OK, let's carry ___on___ ___with___ the meeting.
2　We'll have to finish the meeting now – we've run _____ _____ time.
3　I'll try calling Zhen tomorrow. I couldn't get _____ _____ her this afternoon.
4　At the interview I asked how the job fits _____ _____ the work of other staff.
5　I'm trying to do more exercise and also cut _____ _____ cigarettes.

60.5 Complete this email with these words: *for, in, off, through, to, up.*

Subject	travel details for Paris

Carlos – your flight takes (1) _____ at 9.00 and arrives in Paris at 10.30. You'll have time to check (2) _____ at the hotel and go (3) _____ all the documents one last time. Someone from Richemont will call (4) _____ you at the hotel around 1.30 and take you to their offices. The meeting will take (5) _____ the whole afternoon.
I think that's everything – get back (6) _____ me if you need any more information.

Test 1 Present simple and present continuous

Test 1.1 Underline the correct words.

1 These days our business *goes/is going* really well.
2 *I rarely travel/I'm rarely traveling* abroad in my job.
3 I'll call you back – *I speak/I'm speaking* to a customer right now.
4 Tara is a good friend of mine – *we speak/we're speaking* on the phone every week.
5 Our company *sells/is selling* financial services.
6 At the moment *we develop/we're developing* a new drug to treat arthritis.
7 *I understand/I'm understanding* what you're saying, but I can't agree with you.
8 The new model *weighs/is weighing* less than the old one.

Test 1.2 Put each verb into the present simple (*I do*) or present continuous (*I'm doing*).

1 I _____go_____ (go) to the Paris fashion shows every year.
2 At the moment the dollar _____ (fall) against the euro.
3 The deal isn't agreed yet. We _____ (still/negotiate) about costs.
4 Our factory _____ (operate) 24 hours a day.
5 My name's Bruno and I _____ (come) from Munich.
6 I _____ (stay) at the Marriott Hotel – I'll be there until Friday.

Test 1.3 Put each verb into the present simple or present continuous.

1 Excuse me, _____*do you speak*_____ (you/speak) English?
2 A: I'm here to see Mr. Ivanov.   B: _____ (he/expect) you?
3 What time _____ (the store/open)?
4 This product _____ (not/sell) well at the moment. We're going to withdraw it.
5 What _____ (you/do)? That's not the way to make double-sided photocopies.
6 A: What _____ (you/do)?   B: I'm an accountant.
7 I have worked with Anna in the past, but I _____ (not/know) her very well.
8 _____ (this coat/belong) to you?

Test 1.4 Each sentence contains one mistake of word order. Correct it.

1 The train ~~arrives usually~~ on time. *usually arrives*
2 She rarely is late for work.
3 I go often to Paris on business trips.
4 We should change our supplier – they always are late with deliveries.

Test 2 Past simple and past continuous

Test 2.1 Put the verbs in brackets into the correct form of the past simple (*I did*).

1 A: _____*Did you speak*_____ (you speak) to Susanna about the Firebird project?
   B: Yes. At its last meeting the Board _____ (agree) to go ahead in principle, but
   they _____ (not/decide) on a definite start date.
2 A: Why _____ (he/leave) the company?
   B: The salary _____ (be) too low and the job _____
   (not/offer) him a chance to develop his career.

Test 2.2 Fill in each gap with *at, in, on* or ~ (no preposition).

1 _on_ Tuesday   4 _____ the weekend   7 _____ the end of the month
2 _____ 2005   5 _____ the morning   8 _____ June
3 _____ yesterday   6 _____ last week   9 _____ the second of June

Test 2.3 Write down the past simple (affirmative form only) of the irregular verbs below.

1 become _____   5 know   _____   9   spend _____
2 buy   _____   6 leave _____   10 take   _____
3 feel   _____   7 meet   _____   11 think _____
4 give   _____   8 sell   _____   12 write _____

Test 2.4 In each sentence one verb is in the past simple, and one is in the past continuous. <u>Underline</u> the correct words.

1 I *met/was meeting* Cristina for the first time when we were both in our early twenties – we
   travelled/were travelling together in India.
2 I *sat/was sitting* in the departure lounge of Schiphol Airport when I *looked up/was looking up*
   and saw Mike Ratledge.
3 I'm sorry I *didn't return/wasn't returning* your call earlier – I *showed/was showing* some visitors
   around the building.

Test 2.5 In each sentence, put one verb into the past simple and one into the past continuous.

1 When I _____ (arrive) at my office after lunch, Karen Tweed
   _____ (wait) for me in reception.
2 While I _____ (do) my Masters degree in Finance, I _____ (learn)
   a lot about technical analysis of the markets.

Test 3   Present perfect simple and continuous

Test 3.1   Correct the <u>verb</u> in each sentence so that it has the form of either present perfect or present perfect continuous.

1 <u>You have ever been</u> to China?   *Have you ever been*
2 <u>I'm decided</u> to change jobs. I want more of a challenge.
3 <u>I been feeling ill</u> all morning. I think I'm going home.
4 How long <u>are you working</u> in this company?

Test 3.2   <u>Underline</u> the correct verb form.

1 This week *was/has been* really busy. At least it's over now. See you on Monday!
2 This week *was/has been* really busy – I'm exhausted and it's only Thursday.
3 Here, take my umbrella – *it started/it's started* to rain.
4 And there I was, in the middle of Egypt, in April, and *it started/it's started* to rain!
5 I went to university in Hamburg, but *I live/I've lived* in Stuttgart now.
6 *I live/I've lived* in Stuttgart all my life.
7 There's nothing more to say to them. *We make/We've made* our position clear.
8 We're a small company – *we make/we've made* parts for the automobile industry.

Test 3.3   Complete each sentence with one of these words: *already, ever, for, just, since, ~~yet~~.*

1 I can't join you for lunch. I haven't finished writing this report ____*yet.*____
2 Have you _____ spoken at an international conference?
3 This project has been running _____ March.
4 This project has been running _____ three months.
5 I'm sorry, Mrs Dawson isn't here. She's _____ gone out for a moment.
6 He's only 28 but he's _____ been promoted to Regional Sales Director.

Test 3.4   In each mini-dialogue put one verb into the present perfect and one into the present perfect continuous. Use contractions where possible.

1 A: Ted, come out for some lunch. You _____ (write) that report all morning.
   B: I'll join you in a few minutes. I _____ (nearly/finish) it.
2 A: I'm looking for Claudia. _____ (you see) her?
   B: No, but I _____ (try) to find her as well.
3 A: How long _____ (you/use) iris identification technology?
   B: About two years. We _____ (invest) €2 million in this area.

Test 4 Future forms

Test 4.1 Correct the form of each <u>verb</u>. Forms are: *will, going to* or present continuous.

1 I'm sorry, I won't be here tomorrow. <u>I be</u> in Brussels. *I'll be*

2 <u>I giving</u> a presentation to the Board next week. I'm a bit nervous.

3 What <u>you are going to discuss</u> at the next meeting?

4 Our Chinese visitors <u>will join us probably</u> for lunch.

5 There is a lot to do. <u>Does anyone going to help</u> you?

6 Bye. <u>I see you</u> tomorrow.

Test 4.2 Choose the best reply, a) or b), in each mini-dialogue.

1 Can you help me install some new software this afternoon?
    a) Sorry, I'll meet a client.
    b) Sorry, I'm meeting a client.

2 So, shall we say tomorrow at about 9.30?
    a) OK, I'll see you then.
    b) OK, I'm seeing you then.

3 What are your plans for the product launch?
    a) We invite lots of journalists to a special presentation.
    b) We're going to invite lots of journalists to a special presentation.

4 What about the new deal with our supplier?
    a) I think it'll be good for both sides.
    b) I think it's being good for both sides.

5 It would be nice to see you when you're in Paris next week.
    a) Yes, it would. Are you doing anything on Wednesday evening?
    b) Yes, it would. Will you do anything on Wednesday evening?

Test 4.3 Complete the sentence on the right using only a form of *will* or *be going to* so that it has a similar meaning to the sentence on the left. Use contractions.

1 We plan to redesign the packaging. / We _____*'re going to*_____ redesign the packaging.

2 I promise to call you. / I _____ call you.

3 The weather forecast says rain. / It _____ rain.

4 I'll be absent from the meeting. / I _____ be at the meeting.

5 I've decided to resign. / I _____ resign.

6 I promise not to tell anyone. / I _____ tell anyone.

7 They don't plan to raise prices. / They _____ raise prices.

Test 5 Questions and answers

Test 5.1 Rewrite each sentence as a question.

1   I enjoyed the presentation.   _Did you enjoy the presentation?_
2   They're making a profit.   _____
3   Ruth speaks Spanish.   _____
4   Sales have gone up this month.   _____
5   He's leaving tomorrow.   _____
6   The plane landed on time.   _____
7   The taxi has arrived.   _____
8   They spend a lot of money on R&D.   _____
9   She was expecting an email from them.   _____
10   You've been waiting a long time.   _____
11   The meeting had already started.   _____
12   We should cancel the order.   _____

Test 5.2 Take questions 1–12 that you wrote above and write a short reply beginning as shown.

1   Yes, ____I did.____   5   Yes, _____   9   Yes, _____
2   No, _____   6   No, _____   10   No, _____
3   Yes, _____   7   Yes, _____   11   Yes, _____
4   No, _____   8   No, _____   12   No, _____

Test 5.3 Put the words into the correct order to make questions.

1   When you do start work?   _When do you start work?_
2   What done have you about this fax?   _____
3   When is going to finish the project?   _____
4   How long been you have working here?   _____
5   To where you are going?   _____
6   About what they were talking?   _____
7   Do you know what time is it?   _____
8   Could you tell me where is the station?   _____

Test 5.4 Tick the correct answer each time, a) or b).

1   Who told you?   →   a) I told Sue.   ☐   b) Sue told me.   ☐
2   Who did you tell?   →   a) I told Sue.   ☐   b) Sue told me.   ☐
3   Who do you trust?   →   a) I trust everyone.   ☐   b) Everyone trusts me.   ☐
4   Who trusts you?   →   a) I trust everyone.   ☐   b) Everyone trusts me.   ☐

Test 6 Passives

Test 6.1   Correct the <u>verb</u> in each sentence so that it has a passive form

1   The finished goods <u>are storing</u> in our warehouse.   *are stored*
2   Bernadette <u>was been offered</u> a new job.
3   A new arthritis drug <u>is be tested</u> at the moment.
4   These machines <u>were service</u> last week.
5   Nothing <u>will being decided</u> before next week.
6   Special solvents <u>are adding</u> to the paint to ensure high performance.

Test 6.2   Rewrite each sentence with a passive verb, without mentioning who does the action.

1   We are relaunching this product with a new logo.
    This product _____*is being relaunched*_____ with a new logo.
2   They will finish the construction of our new factory in September.
    The construction of our new factory _____ in September.
3   The Board has chosen a new CEO.
    A new CEO _____
4   We manufacture most of our vehicles in Brazil.
    Most of our vehicles _____ in Brazil.
5   Stelios Haji-Ioannou founded easyJet in 1995.
    easyJet _____ in 1995.
6   We can change the specifications if you want.
    If you want, the specifications _____

Test 6.3   In one example in exercise 2 it is interesting who did the action. Write the passive sentence again, mentioning who did the action:

    _____

Test 6.4   Complete each sentence so that it has a similar meaning to the first. Only mention who does the action if it is interesting or important.

1   Economists expect inflation to rise next year.
    Inflation _____
2   The Chinese invented paper money in the ninth century.
    Paper money _____
3   Cairo is my place of birth.
    I _____ in Cairo.

Test 7   Modal verbs

Test 7.1   Rewrite each sentence, using *can, can't, might* or *must*.

1   Helen knows how to use Excel.

Helen _____ *can use* _____ Excel.

2   I'm sure you're tired after your flight. I'll call you in the morning.

You _____ tired after your flight. I'll call you in the morning.

3   Perhaps I'll see you on Thursday evening.

I _____ you on Thursday evening.

4   I'm sure this isn't the right price.

This _____ the right price.

5   Excuse me, is it all right if I open the window?

Excuse me, _____ the window?

6   I'm not allowed to sign anything unless my boss has agreed.

I _____ anything unless my boss has agreed.

Test 7.2   Put this advice in order 1–4, from unnecessary to urgent action: 1 ☐ 2 ☐ 3 ☐ 4 ☐

a) You could go to the doctor.   c) You should go to the doctor.

b) You must go to the doctor.   d) You don't have to go to the doctor.

Test 7.3   Complete each sentence with one of these words: *could, don't have to, have to, mustn't, should*. If there is more than one answer, choose the best one.

1   We _____ go over the budget – my boss insists.

2   We _____ finish the project on time – my boss insists.

3   You _____ leave a tip – it says that service charge is included.

4   If you want my advice, I think you _____ ask for a transfer to another office.

5   I _____ meet you at your hotel, or at the restaurant. Which would you prefer?

Test 7.4   Complete each sentence with one of these words: *couldn't, didn't have to, might have, must have, should have*. If there is more than one answer, choose the best one.

1   I got a direct flight from Delhi to London, so I _____ change at Dubai.

2   You had to wait six hours at the airport! It _____ been awful for you.

3   You _____ checked with me first before signing the document.

4   Scientists believe that life _____ existed on Mars, but no-one knows for sure.

5   I tried to phone her, but I _____ get through.

Test 8 Conditionals

Test 8.1 Underline the correct words.

1 Usually, if we *make/will make* money, we reinvest it in the business.

2 Things are going well, and if we *make/will make* money this year, we will reinvest it in the business.

3 It's unlikely, but if we *made/will make* any money this year, we would reinvest it in the business.

4 Usually, if we lose money, we *cut/will cut* the advertising budget.

5 Things are going badly, and if we lose money this year, we *cut/will cut* the advertising budget.

6 It's unlikely, but if we lost any money this year, we *will cut/would cut* the advertising budget.

Test 8.2 Complete each sentence as either a first conditional (*If I do …, I will …*) or a second conditional (*If I did …, I would …*). Use contractions where possible.

1 I'm sorry I can't figure out how to use this software. If I _____*had*_____ (have) a manual, I ___*'d be able to*___ (be able to) help you.

2 It's not far. If you _____ (follow) this road, you _____ (come) to the station.

3 I'm not going to accept the offer of a job in Hong Kong. It _____ (be) very difficult for the children if we _____ (move) there.

4 I _____ (be) in Paris at 6 pm if my train _____ (not/be) late.

5 It says 'No Parking'. The police walk past here all the time – if they _____ (see) your car, they _____ (give) you a fine.

6 Communication in this company is terrible. If we _____ (have) regular meetings to share information, we _____ (not/have to) send so many emails.

Test 8.3 Complete one sentence with *unless* and one with *as long as*.

1 We'll agree to give you a discount _____ you increase your order to 1,000 units.

2 _____ you increase your order to 1,000 units, we can't give you a discount.

Test 8.4 Study the example. Then complete the sentences as third conditionals.

If we had increased our order, they would have given us a discount.

1 If you _____ (be) at the presentation, you _____ (enjoy) it.

2 If I _____ (see) my boss yesterday, I _____ (ask) him about your letter.

3 If we _____ (invest) in new technology, we _____ (save) a lot of money.

4 If we _____ (invest) in new technology, we _____ (not/waste) so much money.

5 If I _____ (not/get) a promotion, I think I _____ (look) for another job.

Test 9 Verb patterns

Test 9.1 Underline the correct words.

1 We hope *selling/to sell* 200,000 units per year.
2 The client is very angry and we risk *losing/to lose* their business.
3 Do you mind *coming/to come* back in half an hour?
4 I tried to persuade him, but he refused *listening/to listen*.
5 We didn't finish all the items on the agenda, so we agreed *meeting/to meet* again.
6 The weekend is important to me – I enjoy *spending/to spend* time with my family.
7 I decided *staying/to stay* in a hotel near the airport.
8 Crossing the street in London is terrible – I can't help *looking/to look* the wrong way.
9 We guarantee *supplying/to supply* you with steel at this price for a year.
10 They're so inflexible. There's no point *continuing/to continue* with the negotiations.
11 I suggested *increasing/to increase* the marketing budget, but no-one agreed.
12 She's worked really hard this year – she deserves *getting/to get* a bonus.
13 Unemployment tends *rising/to rise* at this time of year.
14 The job involves *understanding/to understand* a lot of technical information.

Test 9.2 Complete each sentence with the *-ing* form or the *to* + infinitive form of one of these verbs: *be, tell*.

1 I regret _____ my colleagues about my personal problems – it was a big mistake.
2 I regret _____ you that the items you require are no longer available.
3 Remember _____ very careful about what you say – they are our competitors.
4 I remember _____ absolutely amazed the first time I saw the pyramids.

Test 9.3 Tick (✓) the sentence if it is already correct. Add the word *to*, in the right place, if it is not correct.

1 The lawyers advised us check the contract very carefully.
2 Can you bring me a cup of coffee?
3 She was very busy – she asked me come back tomorrow.
4 Emily sends you her best wishes.
5 He promised us a good price.
6 Please remind me call Mrs Banerjee in the morning.
7 Show me the figures.
8 It was a good course – they trained us use Microsoft Office more effectively.
9 I arrived just as the shop was closing. They made me come back the next day.
10 I arrived just as the shop was closing. They let me go in.

Test 10 Reported speech

Test 10.1 Write the actual words that each person says.

1   Ann said that she would be late.

   She said, '_____*I'll be*_____ late.'

2   Dean said he knew about the changes to the invoice.

   Dean said, '_____ about the changes to the invoice.'

3   She said she had sent the shipping confirmation.

   She said, '_____ the shipping confirmation.'

4   Jack said he was coming to the meeting.

   Jack said, '_____ to the meeting.'

5   They asked me at the interview if I could speak French.

   They asked me at the interview, '_____ speak French?'

Test 10.2 Rewrite the sentences in reported speech.

1   'I've lost my passport,' said George.

   George told us that _____*he had lost*_____ his passport.

2   'I'm leaving on Friday,' he said.

   He said that he _____ on Friday.

3   'I'll finish the report as soon as I can,' said Maureen.

   Maureen said that she _____ the report as soon as she _____

4   'Do you have this model in other colours?' the customer asked me.

   The customer asked me if _____ that model in other colours.

5   'Have you made a back-up copy?' the IT guy asked me.

   The IT guy asked me _____ a back-up copy.

6   'How much did you pay for insurance cover?' I asked her.

   I asked her _____ for insurance cover. (2 possible answers)

7   'When is your presentation?' I asked Sue.

   I asked Sue when _____

Test 10.3 <u>Underline</u> the correct words.

1   He *told me/told to me* about the changes in the contract.

2   He *said me/said* there were some changes in the contract.

3   She *promised to give me/promised giving me* some new responsibilities.

4   She *asked me/asked to me* if I would like have some new responsibilities.

5   I *apologized for sending/apologized for to send* the wrong parts.

6   It was lucky that you *reminded me calling/reminded me to call* Nadim.

Test 11 Relative clauses

Test 11.1 <u>Underline</u> the correct words.

1 The train *which/who* goes to Brussels leaves from here.
2 I don't know *which/who* to ask about my job application.
3 Do you know *whose/who* copy of the agenda this is?
4 *That/What* I like best about this job is my colleagues.
5 The companies *that/what* I contacted were not very helpful.
6 Lithuania, *that/which* is the largest Baltic country, has a population of 4 million.

Test 11.2 If the sentence is correct, put a tick (✓). If the sentence has a word which should not be there, cross it out.

1 I'm reading a report that it says the biotechnology market is going to grow rapidly.
2 We use a travel agency which charges a very small commission.
3 We gave the job to someone who has a lot of experience of the German market.
4 My boss is a person who he can take decisions very quickly.

Test 11.3 Combine the sentences using the relative pronoun in brackets.

1 We're going to launch a new line of clothing. It will appeal to teenagers. (that)
   → We're going to launch _____*a new line of clothing that will appeal to teenagers.*_____
2 I share an office with a colleague. She can type at 80 words per minute. (who)
   → I share an office _____
3 I've photocopied the article. It talks about mineral resources in Siberia. (that)
   → I've photocopied _____
4 They've appointed a new Chairman. He comes from the retail industry. (who)
   → They've appointed _____
5 They've appointed a new Chairman. His background is in retailing. (whose)
   → They've appointed _____

Test 11.4 Add one of these prepositions, in the correct place, to each sentence: *for, on, to, with.*

1 These are the points that we should focus in the meeting.
2 The person I report is my line manager, Eleni Kefala.
3 Most of the complaints I deal are about late delivery or faulty products.
4 This is the job that I've applied.

Test 12 Nouns and determiners

Test 12.1 Underline the correct words.

1 I'd like *an/some* information about trains to Kiev.
2 I couldn't find *any/some* information about trains to Kiev.
3 Information about trains to Kiev *is/are* contained in this booklet.
4 There is a lot of *information/informations* about trains to Kiev on the Internet.
5 There is some information on the Internet, but there isn't *many/much*.
6 There's *a few/a little* information about trains to Kiev in this guide book.

Test 12.2 Choose the best alternative, a) or b), to complete each sentence.

1 Let me give you _____
   a) an advice b) some advice
2 Don't worry. _____ plenty of accommodation in Venice at this time of year.
   a) There is b) There are
3 _____ people were off work because of illness yesterday?
   a) How many b) How much
4 Insurance? No, I haven't got _____
   a) some b) any
5 There is _____ to do on my car. It's being serviced at the moment.
   a) a work b) some work
6 We got some new equipment for the office. _____ very expensive.
   a) It was b) They were
7 I couldn't hear the announcement. The hall was full of _____
   a) a noise b) noise
8 The journey was fine. I bought _____ and read it on the train.
   a) a paper b) paper

Test 12.3 Complete each sentence with one of these words: *all, both, either, everyone, neither, no, none.*

1 There are only two candidates, and unfortunately _____ is very good.
2 There are two candidates, and luckily _____ are very good.
3 There are two candidates. We have to choose _____ one or the other.
4 It's very disappointing. _____ of the candidates on this list has an MBA.
5 It's very disappointing. _____ candidate on this list has an MBA.
6 A: Have you interviewed the six candidates?   B: Yes, I've seen _____
7 A: Have you interviewed the six candidates?   B: Yes, I've seen _____ of them.

Test 13 Articles

Test 13.1 <u>Underline</u> the correct words.

1 There's *a/the* woman waiting to see you at *a/the* reception desk.

2 At *an/the* end of *a/the* talk, someone asked *a/the* very difficult question.

3 Hutchison Port Holdings is *a/the* largest shipping line in *a/the* world.

4 When I arrived at *an/the* airport, I had *a/the* coffee and waited for *a/the* flight.

5 It's *an/the* interesting idea. Perhaps we should discuss it at *a/the* meeting on Friday.

6 *A/The* Board agreed to give us *a/the* budget we needed to finish *a/the* project.

7 What's *a/the* difference between *a/the* wholesaler and *a/the* retailer?

8 *A/The* person with *an/the* MBA usually gets *a/the* good job.

9 It's *a/the* way we do things here – whoever sells the most gets *a/the* biggest bonus.

10 I have *a/the* suggestion to make. It's different to *a/the* suggestion I made last week.

11 I have two daughters. One is *a/the* student, and *another/the other* is unemployed.

12 I've got *a/the* German car. It's *a/the* BMW.

Test 13.2 Fill in each space with *the* or ~ (if there is no article).

1 ____~____ discretion and secrecy are very important in ___*the*___ banking industry.

2 I like to drink _____ wine when I go out in _____ evening.

3 _____ company where I used to work produced _____ steel.

4 _____ Dutch are usually very good at speaking _____ English.

5 My company sent me to _____ UK, where I worked for several years. After that I worked for a short time in _____ Belgium, but now I live in _____ Netherlands.

6 We had a great time on our trip to _____ Paris. We stayed at _____ Ritz and saw all the famous sights like the _____ Eiffel Tower and so on.

7 _____ Nile runs from _____ Lake Victoria to _____ Mediterranean.

8 I went trekking in _____ Himalayas and saw _____ Mount Everest.

Test 13.3 Complete each sentence with two words so that it has a similar meaning to the first.

1 Nicola teaches chemistry.

Nicola is _____ teacher.

2 We went to an excellent restaurant last night.

_____ we went to last night was excellent.

3 I didn't expect to see George.

George _____ last person I expected to see.

4 Someone is phoning you.

There's someone on _____

Test 14 Adjectives and adverbs

Test 14.1 Correct the mistake in each sentence.

1 Everyone on the sales team was very happily when the conference finished.

2 At the end of the conference we all felt very tiring.

3 Both sales teams worked well. One was so good as the other.

4 Both sales teams worked well, although on balance team A was better team B.

5 The performance of the sales team was very well.

6 Microsoft are the more successful software company in history.

7 Microsoft are the larger software company in history.

Test 14.2 Complete each sentence with a comparative or superlative form of the adjective in brackets. Include the words *as, more, most, than, the* where necessary.

1 Exxon is _____*the biggest*_____ (big) private oil company in the world.

2 Exxon is _____ (big) ChevronTexaco.

3 The two models are exactly the same size. One is _____ (small) the other.

4 The new model has a fantastic screen – much _____ (good) the old one.

5 It's selling really well. In fact, sales are _____ (good) we've ever seen.

6 This year market conditions will be _____ (difficult) last year.

7 The Emirates Palace in Abu Dhabi is _____ (expensive) hotel in the world.

8 If you want value-for-money, the Z600 is not _____ (expensive) the Z800.

9 The sales figures are not good. They're _____ (bad) last year.

10 The sales figures are a disaster. They're _____ (bad) in our history.

Test 14.3 Complete each sentence so that it has a similar meaning to the first.

1 Could you not talk so fast, please.

Could you talk more ____*slowly*____ , please.

2 It was hard work for everyone.

Everyone worked _____ .

3 I'm a bit tired. I slept badly last night.

I'm a bit tired. I didn't sleep _____ last night.

4 Dell PCs are cheaper than Sony PCs.

Dell PCs are not _____ expensive _____ Sony PCs.

5 Nobody in the company is a better sales consultant than Margarida.

Margarida is _____ _____ sales consultant in the company.

6 Small shops are not as cheap as supermarkets.

Supermarkets are _____ _____ small shops.

Test 15 Linking words

Test 15.1 <u>Underline</u> the correct words.

1 The supermarket sells clothes and household goods *as well/as well as* food.

2 The supermarket sells clothes, household goods and food *as well/as well as*.

3 You weren't in when I called, *so/because* I'm emailing you instead.

4 I'm emailing you *so/because* you weren't in when I called.

5 *Although/Despite* the increase in sales, our market share was smaller.

6 *Although/Despite* sales increased, our market share was smaller.

Test 15.2 Complete each sentence so that it has a similar meaning to the first.

1 Although it was snowing, I arrived at work on time.

Despite *the snow, I arrived at work on time.*

2 Some analysts think that gold is a good investment, but others disagree.

Although some _____

3 Despite putting in a more expensive bid, we won the contract.

Even though we _____

4 I made a lot of useful contacts, although the conference was boring.

Despite the boring _____

Test 15.3 <u>Underline</u> the correct words.

1 He came to me *so that/for* advice.

2 I made a note in my calendar, *so that/in order* I won't forget.

3 I'm here *for/to* see Carol Miller. She's expecting me.

4 I'm here *for/to* the marketing seminar. Can you tell me which room it is?

5 I've called this meeting *for/in order to* discuss the strategic plan.

6 Let's take a taxi *so that/for* we don't have any problems parking.

Test 15.4 Complete each sentence so that it has a similar meaning to the first. Use the word in brackets.

1 I'm going for lunch. (have)

I'm going _____

2 I need to go on vacation to have a rest. (for)

I need to go on _____

3 I might get lost, so I'll take a map. (so that/don't)

I'll take a _____

Test 16 Verb/adjective + preposition

Test 16.1 Decide which preposition from the list goes with each verb.

for (x3)   *in* (x3)   *on* (x3)   *to* (x3)   *with* (x3)

1 You've worked really hard this year. I think you should ask _for_ a pay rise.

2 In markets like China and India we co-operate _____ local partners.

3 If the job is important, ask Sue. You can always rely _____ her.

4 You can achieve most things in life, as long as you believe _____ yourself.

5 To improve your English, you can listen _____ www.bbc.co.uk/worldservice.

6 No, I don't rent my apartment, I own it. It belongs _____ me.

7 I've applied _____ a job at KPMG, but I don't think I'll get it.

8 We specialize _____ the corporate sector, not private individuals.

9 I agree _____ Alberto about this – I think it's a waste of money.

10 In the summer we sell a lot of ice-cream, but of course it depends _____ the weather.

11 Don't worry about the bill, I'll pay _____ it.

12 There's a lot to discuss, so I think we should focus _____ plans for the training day.

13 If the merger goes ahead, what will happen _____ our jobs?

14 He's invested a lot of his own money _____ the company.

15 They say they can supply us _____ all the materials we need.

Test 16.2 Underline the correct preposition.

1 It's an interesting point, but not really relevant *to/with/about* this meeting.

2 Gdansk is famous *of/for/about* its shipyards.

3 The new model is very similar *to/with/of* the old one, only more powerful.

4 Steve is married *for/of/to* Susan.

5 The software is compatible *to/with/for* PCs and Macs.

6 Kate travels by train whenever she can. She's afraid *of/for/with* flying.

7 I'm sorry, I was wrong *for/in/about* Boris. He's actually very nice.

8 Come on! We don't want to be late *with/for/on* the meeting.

9 This model is popular *by/about/with* our younger customers.

10 Can you call me next week? We may be interested *for/in/of* using your services.

11 This paint is suitable *for/to/by* both indoor and outdoor use.

12 My son is typical *to/from/of* teenagers of his age. He just wants to play video games.

13 You look confused. Are you aware *in/of/from* what happened this morning?

14 Angola is rich *in/of/for* all sorts of mineral resources.

15 I've checked all the Powerpoint slides. I think I'm ready *for/to/of* the meeting now.

16 Are you sure our IT system is safe *of/about/from* viruses and hackers?

Test 17 Prepositional phrases

Test 17.1 <u>Underline</u> the correct preposition.

1 The elevator is <u>out of</u>/*without* order; we'll have to take the stairs.
2 There is some office space *at/for* rent in the city centre. The price is very reasonable.
3 The project is going well – we're *at/on* track to finish by the end of July.
4 I'm really *in/with* debt – I've gone up to the limit on all my credit cards.
5 I need to arrive at the meeting early, *in/on* time to do some photocopying.
6 Mr. Ling is *at/on* the other line at the moment – can I ask him to call you back?
7 I think they're delaying the negotiations *by/on* purpose.
8 *At/By* first sight it looks like a good idea, but I need more time to study it.
9 The trains in Switzerland are amazing – they always arrive exactly *in/on* time.
10 Can I call you back tomorrow? I'm really *under/with* pressure right now.
11 I'm sorry, I sent you the wrong documents *by/for* mistake. Can you return them?
12 The colour is *over/up* to you – we can print the leaflet in any colour you want.

Test 17.2 One word or phrase in each group does not go with the preposition. Cross it out.

1 at   a good price/short notice/target
2 by   chance/date/law
3 in   budget/person/touch
4 on   demand/stock/strike
5 in   advance/vacation/writing
6 on   cash/hold/the Internet

Test 17.3 Use one of the correct phrases from Test 17.2 to complete each sentence.

1 After exchanging emails for the last few months, it's nice to finally meet you _____
2 I'm sorry but your order is going to be delayed. The workers in the factory have just gone

   _____

3 Because of the urgent nature of the situation, I had to call this meeting _____
   Thank you for making the time to come.
4 I'm not saying 'yes' and I'm not saying 'no'. Your proposal is _____ and I'll give you
   an answer after we've done some more market research.
5 We have to provide the government with this information. We are obliged _____
   to do it.
6 I think we've covered all the issues now, but I need you to confirm this order _____
   before I can go ahead and process it.

Test 18 Phrasal verbs

Test 18.1 <u>Underline</u> the correct preposition.

    1 I've done some research and I've found *off/<u>out</u>/up* some interesting information.

    2 Microsoft followed a policy of taking *back/over/up* smaller, specialized competitors.

    3 Can you help me? I can't figure *in/off/out* how to use this spreadsheet.

    4 I passed the interview but I turned *back/down/out* the job – the salary was too low.

    5 I'll come to your hotel around eight and pick you *away/out/up* from there.

    6 I left Accenture two years ago to set *away/off/up* my own consultancy company.

    7 Costs are increasing and we won't be able to keep our prices *down/off/out* next year.

    8 Do you think this snow will hold *on/out/up* our flight?

    9 Because of the reorganization the Edinburgh branch is going to close *down/off/out*.

  10 Please draw *down/out/up* a contract, and then I'll ask our lawyers to look at it.

Test 18.2 Rewrite each sentence by replacing the <u>underlined</u> words with one of these phrasal verbs: *deal with, do without, get back to, get over, ~~look after~~, look through.*

    1 Steven usually <u>takes care of</u> the office while I'm away.

        Steven usually _____*looks after*_____ the office while I'm away.

    2 In my job I have to <u>take action in relation to</u> many types of customers.

        In my job I have to _____ many types of customers.

    3 I've <u>searched among</u> the files, but I can't find their details anywhere.

        I've _____ the files, but I can't find their details anywhere.

    4 Lisa is leaving. I don't know how we're going to <u>succeed in working without</u> her.

        Lisa is leaving. I don't know how we're going to _____ her.

    5 He felt bad when he didn't get the promotion, but he's <u>recovered from</u> it now.

        He felt bad when he didn't get the promotion, but he's _____ it now.

    6 Sorry, I'm really busy right now. Can I <u>contact</u> you tomorrow?

        Sorry, I'm really busy right now. Can I _____ you tomorrow?

Test 18.3 Complete each sentence with one of the phrasal verbs: *cut down on, drop in on, get along with, ~~keep up with~~, move on to, run out of.*

    1 I have to read a lot of scientific journals to _____*keep up with*_____ my field.

    2 While we're in Milan, let's _____ Stefano. He'll be pleased to see us.

    3 We've _____ time. We'll discuss the remaining issues at the next meeting.

    4 It's a great place to work. I _____ all my colleagues really well.

    5 I'm getting fat. I'll have to _____ business lunches and start exercising.

    6 OK, that's decided. Shall we _____ the next item on the agenda?

Appendix 1   Regular verbs: formation

Present simple (unit 1)

Affirmative:	*I/you/we/they **work**. She/he/it **works**.*
Question:	***Do** I/you/we/they **work**? **Does** she/he/it **work**?*
Negative:	*I/you/we/they **don't work**. She/he/it **doesn't work**.*

Present continuous (unit 2)

Affirmative:	*I **am working**. You/we/they **are working**. She/he/it **is working**.*
Question:	***Am** I **working**? **Are** you/we/they **working**? **Is** she/he/it **working**?*
Negative:	*I**'m not working**. You/we/they **aren't working**. She/he/it **isn't working**.*

Past simple (unit 4)

Affirmative:	*I/you/she/he/it/we/they **worked**.*
Question:	***Did** I/you/she/he/it/we/they **work**?*
Negative:	*I/you/she/he/it/we/they **didn't work**.*

Past continuous (unit 5)

Affirmative:	*I/she/he/it **was working**. You/we/they **were working**.*
Question:	***Was** I/she/he/it **working**? **Were** you/we/they **working**?*
Negative:	*I/she/he/it **wasn't working**. You/we/they **weren't working**.*

used to (unit 5)

Affirmative:	*I/you/she/he/it/we/they **used to work**.*
Question:	***Did** I/you/she/he/it/we/they **use to work**?*
Negative:	*I/you/she/he/it/we/they **didn't use to work**.*

Present perfect (unit 6)

Affirmative:	*I/you/we/they **have worked**. She/he/it **has worked**.*
Question:	***Have** I/you/we/they **worked**? **Has** she/he/it **worked**?*
Negative:	*I/you/we/they **haven't worked**. She/he/it **hasn't worked**.*

Present perfect continuous (unit 9)

Affirmative:	*I/you/we/they **have been working**. She/he/it **has been working**.*
Question:	***Have** I/you/we/they **been working**? **Has** she/he/it **been working**?*
Negative:	*I/you/we/they **haven't been working**. She/he/it **hasn't been working**.*

Past perfect (unit 10)

Affirmative:	*I/you/she/he/it/we/they* **had worked**.
Question:	**Had** *I/you/she/he/it/we/they* **worked**?
Negative:	*I/you/she/he/it/we/they* **hadn't worked**.

will (unit 12)

Affirmative:	*I/you/she/he/it/we/they* **will work**.
Question:	**Will** *I/you/she/he/it/we/they* **work**?
Negative:	*I/you/she/he/it/we/they* **won't work**.

going to (unit 13)

Affirmative:	*I'm/you're/she's/he's/it's/we're/they're* **going to begin**.
Question:	*Am I/Are you/Is she/Is he/Is it/Are we/Are they* **going to begin**?
Negative:	*I'm not/you aren't/she isn't/we aren't/they aren't* **going to begin**.

Passive (unit 21)

Active	**Passive**
She helps.	*She* **is helped**.
She is helping.	*She* **is being helped**.
She helped.	*She* **was helped**.
She has helped.	*She* **has been helped**.
She will/should help.	*She* **will/should be helped**.

Reported speech (unit 35)

Actual words spoken	**Report**
'I work for IBM.'	*He said (that) he* **worked** *for IBM.*
'I'm working for IBM.'	*He said (that) he* **was working** *for IBM.*
'I took it.'	*He said (that) he* **took** *it/**had taken** it.*
'I've forgotten it.'	*He said (that) he* **had forgotten** *it.*
'I've been reading it.'	*He said (that) he* **had been reading** *it.*
'I will help.'	*He said (that) he* **would** *help.*
'I can help.'	*He said (that) he* **could** *help.*
'I must/should go.'	*He said (that) he* **must/should** *go.*

Appendix 2   Irregular Verbs

Verb	Past simple	Past participle
be	was, were	been
beat	beat	beaten
become	became	become
begin	began	begun
break	broke	broken
bring	brought	brought
broadcast	broadcast	broadcast
build	built	built
buy	bought	bought
catch	caught	caught
choose	chose	chosen
come	came	come
cost	cost	cost
cut	cut	cut
deal	dealt	dealt
do	did	done
draw	drew	drawn
drink	drank	drunk
drive	drove	driven
eat	ate	eaten
fall	fell	fallen
feel	felt	felt
find	found	found
fly	flew	flown
forget	forgot	forgotten
forgive	forgave	forgiven
get	got	got
give	gave	given
go	went	gone
grow	grew	grown
have	had	had
hear	heard	heard
hit	hit	hit
hold	held	held
keep	kept	kept
know	knew	known
lead	led	led

Verb	Past simple	Past participle
learn	learnt/learned	learnt/learned
leave	left	left
lend	lent	lent
let	let	let
lose	lost	lost
make	made	made
mean	meant	meant
meet	met	met
pay	paid	paid
put	put	put
read	read	read
ride	rode	ridden
rise	rose	risen
run	ran	run
say	said	said
see	saw	seen
sell	sold	sold
send	sent	sent
set	set	set
show	showed	shown
shut	shut	shut
sing	sang	sung
sit	sat	sat
sleep	slept	slept
speak	spoke	spoken
spend	spent	spent
stand	stood	stood
take	took	taken
teach	taught	taught
tell	told	told
think	thought	thought
throw	threw	thrown
understand	understood	understood
wake	woke	woken
wear	wore	worn
win	won	won
write	wrote	wrote

Appendix 3   Spelling

Verbs: third person singular of present simple

- To make the third person singular of most verbs we add -*s*. But verbs ending in *o, ch, sh, ss* and *x* add -*es*.

  He goes   She watches   He wishes   She misses   He relaxes

- When the verb ends in consonant + *y*, we remove the -*y* and add -*ies*. But if there is a vowel before the *y* we do not make a change.

  try – he tries   copy – it copies
  BUT *stay – she stays   enjoy – he enjoys*

Verbs: -*ing* form

- We leave out the final -*e* when we add -*ing* to a verb. But we keep a double *e* (*ee*).

  decide – deciding   write – writing
  BUT *see – seeing   agree – agreeing*

- When a verb ends in -*ie*, we change -*ie* to -*ying*.

  die – dying   lie – lying

- Sometimes we double a final consonant. This happens when a verb ends in consonant-vowel-consonant.

  plan – planning   stop – stopping
  BUT *meet – meeting   read – reading   help – helping   work – working*

  With longer verbs (two syllables or more) we only double if the final syllable is stressed.

  begin – beginning   prefer – preferring
  BUT *visit – visiting   remember – remembering*

Verbs: past simple

- To make the past simple of most regular verbs we add -*ed*. But if the verb ends in an -*e* then we just add -*d*.

  work – worked   BUT like – liked

- When a verb ends in consonant + *y*, we remove the -*y* and add -*ied*.

  try – tried   copy – copied

- Sometimes we double a final consonant. This happens when a verb ends in consonant-vowel-consonant.

  plan – planned   stop – stopped

Nouns: plurals

- To make a plural of most nouns we just add -*s*. But nouns ending in -*ch*, -*sh*, -*ss* and -*x* add -*es*.

  match – matches   wish – wishes   glass – glasses   box – boxes

- Most nouns ending in -*o* add -*s*. But a few have -*es*.

  kilos   photos   pianos   studios
  BUT *heroes   potatoes   tomatoes*

- When the noun ends in consonant + *y*, we remove the *-y* and add *-ies*. But if there is a vowel before the *y* we do not make a change.

  party – parties   *story – stories*
  BUT *day – days*   *journey – journeys*

Adverbs

- We form many adverbs by taking the adjective and adding *-ly*. On a few occasions we leave out *e*.

  safe – safely   *strange – strangely*
  BUT *true – truly*   *whole – wholly*

- When the adjective ends in consonant + *y*, we change *-y* to *-ily*.

  easy – easily   *angry – angrily*

- When the adjective ends in consonant + *le*, we change *-e* to *-y*.

  probable – probably   *flexible – flexibly*

- When the adjective ends in *-ic*, we add *-ally*. There is one exception.

  automatic – automatically   *romantic – romantically*
  BUT *public – publicly*

- The suffix *-ful* has only one *l*. When *-ly* is added for adverbs, a double *l* is formed.

  successful – successfully   *hopeful – hopefully*

ie or *ei* ?

- There is a useful rule: *i* before *e*, except after *c*.

  ie   *field*   *believe*
  ei   *receive*

  Exceptions to this rule are *their, weigh* and *weight*.

- If the sound is not /i:/, then we can have *c* followed by *ie*.

  science

q and *u*

- The letter *q* is always followed by *u*.

  question   *require*   *quality*

Silent letters

- Many words contain letters which do not form a sound. These are sometimes called 'silent letters'.

  The silent letters are underlined.

bt	doubt plumber	*ps*	psychology psychiatrist
gn	sign foreign	*sc*	science descend
kn	know knife	*wh*	who why
mb	plumber thumb	*wr*	wrong write

Appendix 4   Punctuation

Capital letters

- Capital letters (also called upper-case letters) are used:

to begin a sentence	*Thank you for your email.*
for names of people	*Patricia, Mr Brady, Mrs Tashiro*
for personal pronoun *I*	*I am sorry it has taken so long to reply.*
for names of organizations	*the United Nations, the Ministry of Finance*
for names of places	*Paris, France, Europe*
for calendar information	*Wednesday, January, New Year's Day*

- Some words can be written with capitals, or in lower-case. These are:

names of the seasons	*in Summer, in summer*
decades	*the Nineties, the nineties*
jobs	*She works in marketing.* (general use)
	She is the Marketing Director. (job title)
points of the compass	*I live in the east of Slovakia.* (general description)
	We operate in the Far East. (place name)

Full stop (.)

- Full stops are used at the end of a sentence.
- They are also used in abbreviations to show that letters in a word are missing. In modern English they are sometimes not used.

  e.g./eg   i.e./ie   etc./etc   Mr./Mr   Mrs./Mrs

Comma (,)

- A comma in writing represents a brief pause in speech. The comma makes the sentence easier to read.

  Total revenue last year was €15 million, and this is a big improvement.
  ~~Total revenue last year was €15 million and this is a big improvement.~~

- A comma is used in lists, except for the last two items where we use *and*.

  This product is available in red, blue, green and black.

  We can use a comma before the final *and* if the last item is a long phrase.

  This product is good quality, easy to clean, and available in a range of colours.

- Linking words at the beginning of a sentence are followed by a comma.

  In fact, total revenues increased last year by 6%.

  Linking words in the middle of a sentence have commas before and after.

  Sales in Latin America, on the other hand, fell slightly last year.

- Commas are used with a non-defining relative clause. (See unit 38.)

  Sales in Brazil, which is an important market for us, increased last year.

- Study where to put a comma with large numbers.

  340   2,900   45,800   750,000   6,500,000

  In some languages a dot is used here. A dot in English represents a decimal point.

- Note that we cannot join two sentences simply by using a comma. Here are two sentences:

Total revenue last year was €15 million. This is a big improvement.

These sentences cannot be joined by just changing the full stop to a comma.

~~Total revenue last year was €15 million, this is a big improvement.~~

But we can join the sentences if we make some small changes. For example:

*Total revenue last year was €15 million, **and** this is a big improvement.*

*Total revenue last year was €15 million, **which** is a big improvement.*

Semi-colon (;)

- We can join two sentences with related meanings using a semi-colon.

The company needs money for investment; this money will come from the bank.

- A semi-colon is used to separate long items in a list. Notice the use of commas and semi-colons in this example:

The companies involved include Novartis, the Swiss pharmaceutical giant; Monsanto, a leading provider of agricultural products; and the German company Bayer.

Colon (:)

- A colon introduces items in a list.

There are three Baltic countries: Estonia, Latvia and Lithuania.

- A colon can introduce an explanation of the previous part of the sentence.

Business is going very well: profits are up, and market share has increased.

- A colon introduces the actual words that someone says.

Last week Emily said to me: 'We need to review our safety procedures.'

Speech marks (' ') (" ")

- Speech marks (also called quotation marks) are used when we write the actual words that someone says. They can be single or double.

My teenage son always says that things are 'boring'.

If we write a whole phrase that someone says, the punctuation goes inside.

'We need to review our safety procedures,' said Emily. (comma inside speech marks)

Emily said: 'We need to review our safety procedures.' (full stop inside speech marks)

- Titles of talks, reports, books, films, etc are put inside single speech marks. Punctuation goes outside.

His presentation was called 'The challenges facing the biotechnology industry'.

Titles like this can also be put in italics rather than speech marks.

Answer key

Grammar terms + test

Exercise 1
1 k 2 c 3 d 4 m 5 b 6 j 7 f 8 a 9 g 10 h
11 i 12 o 13 e 14 n 15 p 16 l

Exercise 2
1 d 2 a 3 g 4 b 5 c 6 h 7 f 8 e

Unit 1 Present simple

Exercise 1.1
1 works 2 doesn't work 3 produces 4 doesn't have
5 do you 6 does he 7 often causes 8 is always 9 I hear
10 you get back

Exercise 1.2
1 dominates 2 employs 3 rules 4 doesn't pay
5 opens 6 close

Exercise 1.3
1 Do you come 2 depends 3 work 4 don't know 5 come
6 do you do 7 direct 8 Do you plan 9 makes 10 do you have
11 needs 12 don't have

Unit 2 Present continuous

Exercise 2.1
1 b 2 c 3 a

Exercise 2.2
1 I'm writing 2 Is he expecting 3 isn't working

Exercise 2.3
1 are becoming 2 is moving 3 is continuing 4 are co-operating

Exercise 2.4
1 are you doing 2 am visiting 3 are developing 4 are you staying
5 is business going 6 isn't doing 7 is becoming 8 aren't reaching

Unit 3 Present simple and present continuous

Exercise 3.1
1 are spending 2 spend 3 am enjoying 4 enjoy 5 raise
6 is raising 7 write 8 is writing 9 are selling 10 sell
11 comes 12 is coming

Exercise 3.2
1 ✓ 2 ✗ 3 ✓ 4 ✗ 5 ✗ 6 ✓ 7 ✗ 8 ✓ 9 ✓ 10 ✗
11 ✓ 12 ✗

Exercise 3.3
1 imagine 2 agree 3 are making 4 am writing 5 are doing
6 remember 7 want 8 are trying 9 need 10 appreciate

Unit 4 Past simple

Exercise 4.1
1 was/went 2 did…know/did…give 3 didn't have/didn't survive

Exercise 4.2
became, began, built, bought, came, developed, got, gave, went, grew,
had, knew, left, made, met, needed, put, sold, took, thought

Exercise 4.3
1 decided/on 2 got/in 3 finished/at 4 put/on 5 renovated/at
6 became/in

Exercise 4.4
1 started 2 sold 3 had 4 grew 5 bought 6 invested
7 began 8 took 9 announced

Unit 5 Past continuous and used to

Exercise 5.1
1 we were trying 2 I wasn't listening 3 were you doing/I was
discussing 4 They weren't wearing/he wasn't driving

Exercise 5.2
1 called/was talking 2 was entering/crashed 3 invented/was
working 4 discovered/was surfing 5 was waiting/arrived
6 started/were building

Exercise 5.3
1 used to take 2 ~ 3 used to have 4 ~ 5 ~ 6 used to own

Unit 6 Present perfect 1

Exercise 6.1
1 been 2 begun 3 bought 4 come 5 done 6 got 7 given
8 gone 9 had 10 known 11 made 12 met 13 seen
14 thought 15 taken 16 written

Exercise 6.2
1 have had 2 has made 3 have begun 4 have been
5 have bought

Exercise 6.3
1 have you heard 2 has announced 3 haven't made
4 have prepared 5 hasn't replied 6 Have you seen

Unit 7 Present perfect 2: time adverbs

Exercise 7.1
1 already 2 yet 3 since 4 never 5 for 6 so far 7 ever
8 just

Exercise 7.2
1 Have you ever been/went 2 Have you ever used/said
3 Have you ever given/wasn't/started

Exercise 7.3
1 for/since 2 since/for 3 for/since

Exercise 7.4
1 yet 2 since 3 already 4 for 5 never 6 Up to now
7 just 8 ever

Unit 8 Present perfect, past simple and present simple

Exercise 8.1
1 b 2 a 3 a 4 b 5 b 6 a

Exercise 8.2
1 started 2 changed 3 has become 4 was 5 has expanded
6 has started

Exercise 8.3
1 went up 2 has gone up 3 goes up 4 I've lived 5 I live
6 I lived 7 I forget 8 I've forgotten 9 I forgot

Exercise 8.4

1 have just come   2 was   3 have invested   4 saw   5 arrived
6 haven't recovered   7 turned   8 have never seen

Unit 9   Present perfect continuous

Exercise 9.1

1 have you been learning   2 has been going up   3 hasn't been
working   4 have been trying   5 Have you been servicing

Exercise 9.2

1 have been looking/have noticed   2 have been making/have invested
3 has lost/has been looking   4 have been emailing/have made

Exercise 9.3

1 ✓   2 ✓   3 ✓   4 ✗   5 ✓   6 ✗

Exercise 9.4

~~I've been asking you/she's been completing~~

Unit 10   Past perfect

Exercise 10.1

I'd been/hadn't heard

3 ✓

Exercise 10.2

1 had left   2 had converted   3 hadn't received   4 had visited
5 hadn't started

Exercise 10.3

1a so I spoke to her colleague instead
1b because she had moved to another company
2a because he had negotiated a better price for some components
2b so I asked him for a pay rise
3a so we decided to look for another supplier
3b because there had been a strike at the factory

Exercise 10.4

1 started   2 had already worked   3 realized   4 had gained
5 left   6 had been

Unit 11   Review of past and present

Exercise 11.1

1 had   2 have never done   3 have known   4 went

Exercise 11.2

1 say   2 are preparing   3 have seen   4 have worked   5 are trying
6 want

Exercise 11.3

1 had already gone   2 was just looking   3 have just had
4 was speaking   5 had heard   6 has been

Unit 12   Future 1: will

Exercise 12.1

1 I'm sure we'll have to   2 I expect we'll have to
3 We'll probably have to   4 We probably won't have to

Exercise 12.2

1 I'll speak to my boss about it.   2 I won't discuss this with anyone.
3 I'll meet you at the station.   4 It's no good – they won't negotiate.
5 Mrs Okada is on another line – will you hold?   6 We need some
fresh air. I'll open a window.   7 If you won't tell him the truth, I will.
8 I won't be here next week. I'll be in Stockholm.

Exercise 12.3

1 c   2 a   3 d   4 b

Exercise 12.4

What will your office look like in twenty years' time? I expect there will
be just a small number of people, sitting on comfortable chairs, talking
together and using hand-held computers. I think more people will
probably work as freelancers, and those still inside the company on
permanent contracts will have more flexible job descriptions. Both
groups will do more work from home, and via the Internet. In general,
companies will be smaller and more specialized. A consequence of all
these trends is that the office will become a place for 'face time' only –
those occasions when meetings of real people are absolutely essential.
But some things probably won't change. These days people want more
and more from their work: they expect their jobs to be more interesting,
creative and satisfying. And I think that this will continue.

Unit 13   Future 2: going to and present continuous

Exercise 13.1

1 prediction   2 plan   3 prediction   4 prediction   5 plan

Exercise 13.2

1 I'm going to look for another job.   2 We're going to patent this
invention.   3 What are you going to do?   4 They aren't going to
have a stand at the Expo.   5 GSK is going to launch a new heart drug.

Exercise 13.3

1 The workforce is going to get older.   2 The trade unions are going to
ask for higher wages.   3 We are not going to have enough time.
4 I think it's going to break down.

Exercise 13.4

1 is coming   2 is she arriving   3 is getting   4 are having
5 Are you taking   6 aren't going

Unit 14   Future 3: review, present simple,
future probability

Exercise 14.1

1 I'm going to visit   2 I'll answer   3 it's going to rain   4 I'll give

Exercise 14.2

1 I'll be   2 I'm arriving   3 I'm having   4 we'll probably continue
5 I'm seeing   6 I'll call

Exercise 14.3

1 will rise/announce   2 arrive/will call   3 will turn off/leave
4 upgrade/will be able to   5 pay/will have

Exercise 14.4

1 is unlikely to   2 is certain to   3 is likely to

Unit 15   Questions 1: yes/no questions

Exercise 15.1

1 Does Bill think it's a good idea?   2 Is Sonia arriving on Monday?
3 Did he make a copy of the Excel file?   4 Have they offered her the
job?   5 Will she be at the meeting tomorrow?

Exercise 15.2

1 Were you reading about IBM?   2 Do most servers use Linux?
3 Is the popularity of Linux falling?   4 Did Linux start in the eighties?
5 Have you installed it on your computers?   6 Has the inventor been
making a lot of money?

Exercise 15.3

1 I did.   2 I haven't.   3 I do.   4 he doesn't.   5 I did.   6 I can't.
7 I am.   8 she isn't.

Exercise 15.4

1 Did   2 Are   3 Have   4 does   5 do   6 has   7 Is

Unit 16   Questions 2: yes/no answers

Exercise 16.1

1 right   2 course/ahead   3 Actually   4 kind   5 appreciate
6 asking   7 afraid   8 honest

Exercise 16.2

1(+) a 1(-) f   2(+) b 2(-) e   3(+) d 3(-) g   4(+) c 4(-) h

Exercise 16.3

1 I'm fine.   2 Yes, of course.   3 Yes. that's right.   4 Actually
5 I know what you're saying   6 That's just not possible.

Unit 17   Questions 3: wh- and how questions

Exercise 17.1

1 did you talk about   2 does a hybrid car work   3 did Berkshire
Hathaway make   4 is Ford's market share falling   5 Which Vice-
President   6 What advice   7 Whose bag is this   8 What type of
loan are you interested in

Exercise 17.2

1 do you get to work?   2 are you staying?   3 did you pay for the
flight?   4 have you interviewed?   5 have you been waiting?
6 will you have?

Exercise 17.3

1 How many   2 How big   3 How often   4 How far   5 How long
6 How fast

Exercise 17.4

Line 1: what your name is   Line 2: what are you doing   Line 3: What
did you do   Line 4: How long have you been   Line 5: responsibilities
have you had   Line 6: why do you want

Unit 18   Questions 4: subject/object and indirect questions

Exercise 18.1

1 met you   2 did you meet   3 started Microsoft   4 did Microsoft
start 5 spoke   6 did she speak   7 happened   8 did it happen
9 told you   10 did you tell

Exercise 18.2

1 b   2 a   3 d   4 c   5 e   6 f   7 h   8 g   9 j   10 i

Exercise 18.3

1 did you make?   2 made 50% of the total?   3 did you launch?
4 has 6% market share?   5 resigned?   6 went missing?
7 did he use?   8 did the police find him?

Exercise 18.4

1 where the ticket office is?   2 how much the ticket costs?
3 when the train leaves?   4 which platform it is?   5 if I have to
change trains?   6 if I'm in the right seat?

Unit 19   Time expressions 1

Exercise 19.1

1 h   2 j   3 f   4 b   5 e   6 d   7 a   8 c   9 i   10 g

Exercise 19.2

1 UK   2 USA   3 UK   4 USA   5 UK   6 USA
Birthday example 31 August 1984.
British style: 31/8/84   American style: 8/31/84

Exercise 19.3

1 at   2 in   3 in   4 on   5 on   6 in   7 in   8 on   9 at   10 on
11 on   12 at

Exercise 19.4

Present simple: every week, once a year, usually
Present continuous: at the moment, currently, nowadays, these days
Past simple: ago, last week, yesterday
Present perfect: already, not yet, since, so far this year, up to now

Unit 20   Time expressions 2

Exercise 20.1

1 for   2 during   3 three months ago   4 since January
5 for three months   6 nowadays

Exercise 20.2

1 ago   2 for   3 since   4 nowadays   5 in

Exercise 20.3

1 by   2 in time   3 on time   4 until   5 by

Exercise 20.4

1 on time   2 by   3 in time   4 At last   5 until

Unit 21   Passive 1

Exercise 21.1

1 made   2 has been closed   3 is being modernized   4 was created
5 will be paid   6 is done

Exercise 21.2

1 are imported   2 is being reorganized   3 was founded
4 have been disappointed

Exercise 21.3

1 ~~by a technician~~   2 ✓   3 ~~by people~~   4 ✓   5 ~~by someone~~

Exercise 21.4

1 are targeted   2 is seen   3 is being caused   4 are being replaced

Unit 22   Passive 2

Exercise 22.1

1 will be seen   2 was given   3 was given a copy of the report by
4 is expected to rise   5 are thought to be   6 was born

Exercise 22.2

1 need   2 are ground   3 are placed   4 contains   5 heat
6 is forced   7 falls   8 should be cleaned

Exercise 22.3

First/Then/Next/Finally

Exercise 22.4

1 have been treated   2 should be referred   3 must be scheduled
4 can be invited

ANSWER KEY

Unit 23   Modal verbs 1: ability and requests

Exercise 23.1
1 Can you come   2 I can come   3 I can't come   4 I will be able to
5 I couldn't   6 I wasn't able to   7 can we have   8 we meet
9 meeting   10 Could you

Exercise 23.2
1 Could you wait for me?/Would you wait for me?   2 Could I ask who
is calling?/May I ask who is calling?   3 Could you repeat that?/Would
you repeat that?   4 Could I interrupt you?/May I interrupt you?

Exercise 23.3
1 I call a taxi?   2 we go to that new Italian restaurant?   3 we go for
a drink after work?   4 I call back tomorrow?

Exercise 23.4
1 Would you   2 Shall I   3 may I   4 would you

Unit 24   Modal verbs 2: obligation and necessity

Exercise 24.1
1 should   2 don't have to   3 have to   4 shouldn't   5 can't
6 mustn't

Exercise 24.2
1 don't have to   2 mustn't   3 must   4 have to   5 should
6 shouldn't   7 can   8 can't

Exercise 24.3
1 need to   2 can't   3 can   4 don't have to

Unit 25   Modal verbs 3: probability

Exercise 25.1
1 b   2 c   3 a

Exercise 25.2
1 must be   2 could be   3 might be   4 may not have   5 could be
6 might rain   7 can't be   8 shouldn't rise   9 must be
10 may not come   11 must be   12 can't be

Exercise 25.3
1 may   2 must   3 might not   4 won't

Exercise 25.4
1 might be   2 must be   3 can't be   4 shouldn't be

Unit 26   Modal verbs 4: modals in the past

Exercise 26.1
1 could/was able to   2 was able to   3 could/were able to
4 was able to

Exercise 26.2
1 shouldn't have gone   2 didn't have to go   3 should have gone
4 had to go

Exercise 26.3
1 a   2 c   3 f   4 b   5 d   6 e

Exercise 26.4
1 could have   2 should have   3 can't have   4 must have
5 might not have

Unit 27   Conditionals 1: zero and first conditional

Exercise 27.1
1 b   2 a   3 a   4 b   5 b   6 a

Exercise 27.2
1 speaks/mentions   2 speaks/will mention   3 I do/I make
4 We'll be/we aren't   5 we don't reach/they'll walk away
6 I use/there's   7 you see/send her   8 you order/send

Exercise 27.3
1 there's   2 we'll lose   3 we lose   4 we won't be able
5 our customers aren't   6 they'll go   7 we don't negotiate
8 there'll be

Unit 28   Conditionals 2: second conditional

Exercise 28.1
1 reduced/would go   2 worked/would support   3 I'd take/I were
4 weren't   5 could/would   6 get

Exercise 28.2
1 a   2 b   3 b   4 a   5 a   6 b

Exercise 28.3
1 worked   2 would be   3 wouldn't be   4 earned
5 wouldn't matter   6 would happen   7 didn't like   8 didn't work
9 wouldn't keep   10 had

Unit 29   Conditionals 3: more conditional clauses

Exercise 29.1
1 a   2 b   3 b   4 a   5 b   6 a

Exercise 29.2
1 unless we get a bank loan   2 unless it's urgent   3 unless they offer
me a better salary   4 won't finish the project on time

Exercise 29.3
1 in case I forget it   2 in case my laptop stops working
3 in case their documents aren't in order

Exercise 29.4
1 c   2 d   3 a   4 b

Unit 30   Conditionals 4: third conditional

Exercise 30.1
1 had told/would have done   2 had known/wouldn't have invested
3 had used/would have been   4 would have won/had made

Exercise 30.2
1 had got/wouldn't have missed   2 had known/would have made
3 hadn't booked/wouldn't have got   4 had had/wouldn't have lost

Exercise 30.3
1 had asked   2 would have been   3 hadn't been
4 would have done   5 wouldn't have gone   6 had known

Exercise 30.4
1 hadn't dealt/wouldn't be   2 hadn't dealt/wouldn't have lost
3 had gone/would know

Unit 31   Verbs followed by *-ing* or to + infinitive 1

Exercise 31.1
1 to be   2 extending   3 to have   4 losing   5 postponing
6 to spend   7 to prepare   8 waiting   9 to advertise   10 wasting

Exercise 31.2
1 to negotiate   2 to catch   3 writing   4 advertising   5 to receive
6 auditing   7 designing   8 to replace

Exercise 31.3

1 introducing   2 to prepare   3 getting   4 standing   5 to pay
6 giving   7 dealing   8 to have

Unit 32   Verbs followed by -ing or to + infinitive 2

Exercise 32.1

1 b   2 a   3 a   4 b   5 b   6 a

Exercise 32.2

1 ✓   2 ✓   3 ✓   4 ✗   5 ✗   6 ✓

Exercise 32.3

1 to open   2 opening   3 seeing   4 to give   5 to meet
6 meeting   7 calling   8 to get

Exercise 32.4

1 being   2 to go   3 to find   4 to paying   5 using

Unit 33   Verbs and objects

Exercise 33.1

1 ✗   2 ✓   3 ✓   4 ✗   5 ✓   6 ✗   7 ✗   8 ✓   9 ✓   10 ✗   11 ✓
12 ✗   13 ✓   14 ✗   15 ✗   16 ✓   17 ✗   18 ✓   19 ✓   20 ✗

Exercise 33.2

2 ✓   6 ✓

Exercise 33.3

1 She helped me to install the software.
2 They have invited me to speak at the conference.
3 He warned me not to park there.
4 Could you remind me to call Head Office later.
5 They trained us to maintain the new machines.
6 She encouraged me to apply for the job.

Exercise 33.4

to go on vacation (line 7)   to see your point of view (line 10)
to decide too quickly (line 16)   to wait (line 16)
to buy something (line 17)

Unit 34   The -ing form

Exercise 34.1

1 c   2 e   3 f   4 a   5 b   6 d

Exercise 34.2

1 shopping   2 selling   3 charming   4 increasing   5 meeting

Exercise 34.3

1 surprising   2 surprised   3 fascinated   4 fascinating   5 hearing
6 hear   7 work   8 working

Exercise 34.4

1 retiring   2 finishing   3 relying   4 paying   5 producing
6 continuing

Unit 35   Reported speech 1

Exercise 35.1

1 had seen   2 that morning   3 didn't agree   4 could see
5 were spending

Exercise 35.2

1 I've contacted   2 I'll be   3 I'm going to process   4 I want to check

Exercise 35.3

1 was/the next day   2 would/me   3 they/our/before   4 there/that/was

Exercise 35.4

1 she wasn't sure when she'd arrive.
2 was finishing some paperwork and he wouldn't be long.
3 she didn't think it could be repaired but she'd do her best.

Unit 36   Reported speech 2

Exercise 36.1

1 said   2 told me   3 said   4 said to Maria

Exercise 36.2

1 advised me to take more exercise.   2 apologized for missing the
presentation.   3 refused to renegotiate the contract.   4 reminded me
(us/him/her) to back up all the files.   5 suggested extending the
Christmas sale by a week.   6 promised to be at the meeting on Friday.
7 told Robert (that) he was fired.

Exercise 36.3

1 if I spoke French.   2 if I was prepared to relocate to France.
3 if I could use Microsoft Office.   4 if I was hoping for a salary increase.

Exercise 36.4

1 what the real problem at EuroCom was.   2 what the auditors had
discovered.   3 when they could see the auditors' report.   4 how much
money investors would lose.   5 what he was going to do next.

Unit 37   Relative clauses 1

Exercise 37.1

1 whose   2 which/that   3 who/that

Exercise 37.2

1 who   2 which   3 whose   4 which   5 who   6 whose

Exercise 37.3

1 ✓   2 it   3 she   4 ✓   5 its

Exercise 37.4

1 a new financial product that is aimed at wealthy clients.   2 a new
job that is very stressful.   3 a translator who can speak Lithuanian and
Polish.   4 a cell phone that can connect directly to our network.
5 a new client who could give us a lot of business.

Unit 38   Relative clauses 2

Exercise 38.1

1 went to the conference with   2 bought my printer from
3 we are interested in   4 I am responsible for   5 I was looking at
6 you need to talk to

Exercise 38.2

1 the company where   2 exactly what you want   3 the laboratory
where we do   4 interested in what she was saying   5 the region
where most of our cork   6 we can ship what you need

Exercise 38.3

Advanced Micro Devices (AMD), which has taken second place to Intel
for many years, wants to become a major competitor in the
microprocessor business. Its Chief Executive Hector de Jesus Ruiz, who is
a Mexican immigrant with a PhD in electronics, hopes to use AMD's
success in the server market to convince customers to buy PCs and
notebooks containing AMD semiconductors. But both AMD and Intel
will find it difficult to make money in the PC market, which has been
growing very slowly in recent years. They need to target new areas such
as digital TVs, set-top boxes and cell phones. But in the end, the battle
between AMD and Intel will depend on marketing as much as
technology. Intel have recently appointed Eric Kim, who used to be

Samsung's top marketing exec, to make its brand more exciting and broaden its marketing message.

Unit 39   Countable and uncountable nouns 1

Exercise 39.1

1 a/some   2 some/a   3 some/an   4 a/some   5 a/some   6 some/a
7 some/a   8 an/some   9 some/a   10 some/a   11 a/some
12 a/some

Exercise 39.2

1 is   2 are   3 is   4 are   5 is   6 is   7 are

Exercise 39.3

1 much   2 many   3 is   4 are   5 some   6 a few   7 a little
8 many   9 are   10 some

Unit 40   Countable and uncountable nouns 2

Exercise 40.1

1 a business   2 Business   3 work   4 a work   5 Life   6 a life
7 experience   8 an experience   9 a glass   10 glass

Exercise 40.2

1 are   2 is/are   3 is   4 is/are   5 is/are   6 are

Exercise 40.3

1 c   2 a   3 d   4 f   5 b   6 e

Exercise 40.4

1 a glass   2 glass   3 a paper   4 paper   5 wood   6 a wood
7 an iron   8 iron   9 fish   10 a fish

Unit 41   Determiners 1

Exercise 41.1

1 any some customers   2 ✓   3 ✓   4 some any swordfish
5 any some really interesting people   6 some any serious complaints
7 ✓   8 some any precious metals

Exercise 41.2

1 some   2 any   3 any   4 some

Exercise 41.3

1 How much   2 How many   3 a few   4 a little   5 much   6 many
7 a lot of

Exercise 41.4

1 much   2 a few   3 many   4 a little

Unit 42   Determiners 2

Exercise 42.1

1 all of us   2 All the sales reps   3 Some countries   4 Everything
5 none of the files   6 no messages   7 any end   8 every option
9 each one   10 both days   11 neither of us   12 either

Exercise 42.2

1 Neither/is   2 Every/is   3 None/of   4 any   5 both   6 either

Exercise 42.3

1 Both   2 each   3 neither   4 none   5 either   6 no

Unit 43   Articles 1

Exercise 43.1

1 a/the   2 The/an   3 a/the   4 a/The   5 The/a   6 a/the

Exercise 43.2

1A: an   1B: the   2A: the   2B: a   3A: a   3B: The   4A: the   4B: a

Exercise 43.3

1 an/the   2 The/a   3 the/an   4 a/the   5 The/a   6 a/the

Exercise 43.4

1 a   2 the   3 a   4 an   5 the   6 the   7 a   8 the

Unit 44   Articles 2

Exercise 44.1

1a) ✓   2a) ✓   3b) ✓   4b) ✓   5a) ✓   6a) ✓   7a) ✓
Corrections: 1b) the money   2b) The Shares   3a) The profits
4a) the people   5b) The meat   6b) The Management
7b) The Liberty, The Equality, The Fraternity

Exercise 44.2

1 The English   2 ✓   3 the most important person   4 ✓

Exercise 44.3

1 ~   2 the   3 the   4 ~   5 the

Exercise 44.4

1 ~   2 the   3 the   4 ~   5 the   6 ~   7 the   8 ~

Unit 45   Possessives

Exercise 45.1

1 our   2 ours   3 my   4 mine   5 their   6 yours   7 my
8 yours   9 its   10 hers

Exercise 45.2

1 their   2 theirs   3 yours   4 your   5 hers   6 her

Exercise 45.3

1 = is   2 possession   3 = has

Exercise 45.4

Felix – it's time to start planning the Frankfurt Trade Fair. I thought I'd start by looking at last year's report, which was written by Lena. It says that our stand was very attractive visually, but our main competitor's stand had more people working on it, giving out brochures, etc. In terms of numbers, their stand was visited by approximately 20% more people than ours. Lena organized everything last time, but this year she's very busy, and anyway I think it's someone else's turn, not hers. What about Andreas Kofler from the Stuttgart office? Andreas's input to the planning of the sales conference last March was very good – should we ask him to take responsibility?

Unit 46   Pronouns

Exercise 46.1

1 hurt yourself   2 change   3 feel   4 enjoyed ourselves   5 sit down   6 taught myself   7 help yourselves   8 complained
9 woke up   10 introduce myself

Exercise 46.2

1 anyone   2 nothing   3 everywhere   4 No one   5 Someone
6 anything   7 anything   8 everyone

Exercise 46.3

1 nothing   2 something   3 anything   4 everything

Exercise 46.4

1 someone   2 anyone   3 everyone   4 no one

Unit 47   It's and there's

Exercise 47.1

1 There's/It   2 It's/there are   3 It/there   4 There/there are
5 It's/there is   6 There/It   7 there's/It   8 It's/there are
9 It's/there are   10 it/it's/There are/it/it's

Exercise 47.2

1 have you got   2 I've got   3 Is there   4 there isn't   5 There's
6 she's got   7 I don't have   8 Have you got   9 I haven't got
10 There are

Unit 48   Adjectives and adverbs

Exercise 48.1

1 improved gradually.   2 recovered slowly.   3 collapsed dramatically.
4 increased slightly.

Exercise 48.2

1 quickly   2 fast   3 late   4 unexpectedly   5 efficiently   6 hard

Exercise 48.3

1 The demand for oil is growing considerably all over the world right
now.   2 She's done well in her career in recent years.

Exercise 48.4

1 well/good   2 good/well   3 well/good

Exercise 48.5

1 important   2 heavily   3 great   4 fantastic   5 high
6 specifically   7 exactly   8 light

Unit 49   Comparison 1: adjectives

Exercise 49.1

2 profitable/more profitable than   3 safe/the safest   4 big/bigger
than   5 riskier than/the riskiest   6 good/the best   7 bad/the worst
8 more powerful than/the most powerful   9 newer than/the newest
10 far/the furthest

Exercise 49.2

1 the most exciting   2 worse   3 more and more   4 more   5 It's
6 It isn't

Exercise 49.3

1 most famous   2 faster   3 more functional   4 closest   5 as good
6 more successful   7 smaller   8 smaller   9 trendier   10 more
exciting   11 greatest   12 coolest

Unit 50   Comparison 2: adverbs and nouns

Exercise 50.1

1 longer than   2 more loudly   3 more efficiently   4 better
5 twice as much   6 as

Exercise 50.2

1 more   2 less   3 as much   4 as many   5 fewer

Exercise 50.3

1 slightly   2 much   3 twice   4 not nearly

Unit 51   Degree

Exercise 51.1

1 too low   2 high enough   3 too quickly   4 carefully enough
5 enough time   6 too much   7 too many   8 enough employees

Exercise 51.2

1 such a   2 so   3 such   4 so   5 such   6 such a

Exercise 51.3

1 so many   2 so much   3 so little   4 so few   5 too late   6 so late

Exercise 51.4

1 so many   2 such a   3 so much   4 so   5 too many   6 not enough

Unit 52   Linking words 1

Exercise 52.1

1 too   2 as well as   3 Despite   4 so   5 despite   6 although
7 because   8 so   9 in spite of   10 As

Exercise 52.2

1 We offer good quality as well as cheap prices.
2 My English is quite good because I lived in London for two years.
3 I lived in London for two years so my English is quite good.
4 I like my job even though it's not well-paid.
5 It was getting late so I decided to go home.
6 As it was getting late, I decided to go home.

Exercise 52.3

1 as well   2 even though   3 as   4 so   5 In spite of

Unit 53   Linking words 2

Exercise 53.1

1 Secondly/However   2 For instance/In addition   3 However/Therefore
4 In fact/Bascially

Exercise 53.2

1 ✓   2 ✗   3 ✓   4 ✓   5 ✓   6 ✗

Exercise 53.3

1 As a result   2 Actually   3 Besides this   4 On the other hand
5 Taking everything into consideration

Unit 54   Linking words 3

Exercise 54.1

1 for   2 to have   3 for telephoning   4 In order to   5 so   6 to
7 for   8 so that   9 to   10 for recording

Exercise 54.2

1 to   2 so that   3 for   4 so that   5 for   6 to

Exercise 54.3

1 like/as   2 like   3 like/as if   4 as

Exercise 54.4

1 to   2 for   3 like   4 so that   5 as

Unit 55   Verb + preposition

Exercise 55.1

1 to   2 on   3 to   4 with   5 on   6 of   7 on   8 of   9 to   10 on

Exercise 55.2

1 apologize to   2 apologize for   3 agree with   4 agree to
5 hear from   6 heard about

Exercise 55.3

1 Who does this belong to?   2 ✓   3 ✓
4 What is this going to lead to?

Exercise 55.4

1 in   2 on   3 for   4 against   5 for   6 with

Unit 56   Adjective + preposition

Exercise 56.1

1 c   2 a   3 e   4 b   5 h   6 d   7 f   8 g

Exercise 56.2

1 suitable for   2 rich in   3 attached to   4 safe from   5 aware of

Exercise 56.3

1 with   2 about   3 for   4 at   5 for   6 to

Exercise 56.4

1 in   2 for   3 with   4 to   5 about   6 at   7 of   8 on

Unit 57   Prepositional phrases

Exercise 57.1

1 at   2 by/on   3 by/in   4 At/in   5 By/on   6 out of/in   7 on/in
8 on/in

Exercise 57.2

1 ~~in trouble~~   2 ~~on order~~   3 ~~out of stock~~   4 ~~in the end~~   5 ~~by hand~~
6 ~~up to you~~   7 ~~on business~~   8 ~~in writing~~   9 ~~on order~~   10 ~~on business~~

Exercise 57.3

1 in   2 on   3 at   4 under   5 at   6 on   7 on   8 on   9 by   10 up

Unit 58   Prepositions of place

Exercise 58.1

1 in   2 at   3 on   4 in   5 on   6 at

Exercise 58.2

1 on   2 in   3 at   4 in   5 on   6 in   7 at   8 on   9 on   10 in

Exercise 58.3

1 over   2 above   3 below   4 under

Exercise 58.4

1 at   2 in   3 on   4 in   5 on   6 at   7 at   8 on

Unit 59   Phrasal verbs 1: separable

Exercise 59.1

1 ~~set up it~~   2 ~~fill in it~~   3 ~~turn off it~~   4 ~~pick up me~~

Exercise 59.2

1 b   2 d   3 f   4 c   5 a   6 e

Exercise 59.3

1 close   2 put   3 draw   4 take

Exercise 59.4

1 out   2 up   3 out   4 up   5 off

Unit 60   Phrasal verbs 2: inseparable

Exercise 60.1

1 b   2 c   3 a

Exercise 60.2

1 d   2 a   3 b   4 c

Exercise 60.3

1 The lift has broken down.   2 How are you getting on?
3 The negotiations have fallen through.   4 Inflation is coming down.
5 Hold on a moment while I find a pen.

Exercise 60.4

1 on with   2 out of   3 through to   4 in with   5 down on

Exercise 60.5

1 off   2 in   3 through   4 for   5 up   6 to

Test 1 Present simple and present continuous

Test 1.1

1 is going 2 I rarely travel 3 I'm speaking 4 we speak 5 sells
6 we're developing 7 I understand 8 wieghs

Test 1.2

1 go 2 is falling 3 are still negotiating 4 operates 5 come
6 am staying

Test 1.3

1 do you speak 2 Is he expecting 3 does the store open
4 isn't selling 5 are you doing 6 do you do 7 don't know
8 Does this coat belong

Test 1.4

1 usually arrives 2 is rarely 3 often go 4 are always

Test 2 Past simple and past continuous

Test 2.1

1 Did you speak/agreed/didn't decide 2 did he leave/was/didn't offer

Test 2.2

1 on 2 in 3 ~ 4 at 5 in 6 ~ 7 at 8 in 9 on

Test 2.3

1 became 2 bought 3 felt 4 gave 5 knew 6 left 7 met
8 sold 9 spent 10 took 11 thought 12 wrote

Test 2.4

1 met/were travelling 2 was sitting/looked up 3 didn't return/was
showing

Test 2.5

1 arrived/was waiting 2 was doing/learnt (or learned)

Test 3 Present perfect simple and continuous

Test 3.1

1 Have you ever been 2 I've decided 3 I've been feeling
4 have you been working

Test 3.2

1 was 2 has been 3 it's started 4 it started 5 I live 6 I've lived
7 We've made 8 we make

Test 3.3

1 yet 2 ever 3 since 4 for 5 just 6 already

Test 3.4

1 've been writing/'ve nearly finished 2 Have you seen/'ve been trying
3 have you been using/'ve invested

Test 4 Future forms

Test 4.1

1 I'll be 2 I'm giving 3 are you going to discuss
4 will probably join us 5 Is anyone going to help 6 I'll see you

Test 4.2

1 b 2 a 3 b 4 a 5 a

Test 4.3

1 're going to 2 'll 3 's going to 4 won't 5 'm going to
6 won't 7 're not going to (or aren't going to)

Test 5 Questions

Test 5.1

1 Did you enjoy the presentation? 2 Are they making a profit?
3 Does Ruth speak Spanish? 4 Have sales gone up this month?
5 Is he leaving tomorrow? 6 Did the plane land on time?
7 Has the taxi arrived? 8 Do they spend a lot of money on R&D?
9 Was she expecting an email from them? 10 Have you been waiting
a long time? 11 Had the meeting already started? 12 Should we
cancel the order?

Test 5.2

1 I did 2 they aren't (they're not) 3 she does 4 they haven't
5 he is 6 it didn't 7 it has 8 they don't 9 she was
10 I haven't 11 it had 12 we shouldn't

Test 5.3

1 When do you start work?
2 What have you done about this fax?
3 When is the project going to finish?
4 How long have you been working here?
5 Where are you going to?
6 What were they talking about?
7 Do you know what time it is?
8 Could you tell me where the station is?

Test 5.4

1 b 2 a 3 a 4 b

Test 6 Passives

Test 6.1

1 are stored 2 has been offered 3 is being tested 4 were serviced
5 will be decided 6 are added

Test 6.2

1 is being relaunched 2 will be finished 3 has been chosen
4 are manufactured 5 was founded 6 can be changed

Test 6.3

easyJet was founded by Stelios Haji-Ioannou in 1995.

Test 6.4

1 is expected to rise next year 2 was invented by the Chinese in the
ninth century 3 was born

Test 7 Modal verbs

Test 7.1

1 can use 2 must be 3 might see 4 can't be 5 can I open
6 can't sign

Test 7.2

1 d 2 a 3 c 4 b

Test 7.3

1 mustn't 2 have to 3 don't have to 4 should 5 could

Test 7.4

1 didn't have to 2 must have 3 should have 4 might have
5 couldn't

ANSWER KEY

Test 8   Conditionals

Test 8.1
1 make   2 make   3 made   4 cut   5 will cut   6 would cut

Test 8.2
1 had/'d be able   2 follow/'ll come   3 would be ('d be)/moved
4 'll be/isn't   5 see/'ll give   6 had/wouldn't have to

Test 8.3
1 as long as   2 Unless

Test 8.4
1 had been/would have enjoyed   2 had seen/would have asked
3 had invested/would have saved   4 had invested/wouldn't have
wasted   5 hadn't got/would have looked

Test 9   Verb patterns

Test 9.1
1 to sell   2 losing   3 coming   4 to listen   5 to meet   6 spending
7 to stay   8 looking   9 to supply   10 continuing   11 increasing
12 to get   13 to rise   14 understanding

Test 9.2
1 telling   2 to tell   3 to be   4 being

Test 9.3
1 to check   2 ✓   3 to come back   4 ✓   5 ✓   6 to call   7 ✓
8 to use   9 ✓   10 ✓

Test 10   Reported speech

Test 10.1
1 I'll be   2 I know   3 I've sent (or I'd sent)   4 I'm coming
5 Can you

Test 10.2
1 had lost   2 was leaving   3 would finish/could   4 we (I) had
5 if I had made   6 how much she paid (had paid)   7 her presentation
was

Test 10.3
1 told me   2 said   3 promised to give me   4 asked me
5 apologized for sending   6 reminded me to call

Test 11   Relative clauses

Test 11.1
1 which   2 who   3 whose   4 What   5 that   6 which

Test 11.2
1 it   2 ✓   3 ✓   4 he

Test 11.3
1 a new line of clothing that will appeal to teenagers.
2 with a colleague who can type at 80 words per minute.
3 the article that talks about mineral resources in Siberia.
4 a new Chairman who comes from the retail industry.
5 a new Chairman whose background is in retailing.

Test 11.4
1 we should focus on   2 I report to   3 I deal with   4 I've applied for

Test 12   Nouns and determiners

Test 12.1
1 some   2 any   3 is   4 information   5 much   6 a little

Test 12.2
1 b   2 a   3 a   4 b   5 b   6 a   7 b   8 a

Test 12.3
1 neither   2 both   3 either   4 None   5 No   6 everyone   7 all

Test 13   Articles

Test 13.1
1 a/the   2 the/the/a   3 the/the   4 the/a/the   5 an/the
6 The/the/the   7 the/a/a   8 A/an/a   9 the/the   10 a/the
11 a/the other   12 a/a

Test 13.2
1 ~/the   2 ~/the   3 The/~   4 The/~   5 the/~/the   6 ~/the/the
7 The/~/the   8 the/~

Test 13.3
1 a chemistry   2 The restaurant   3 was the   4 the phone

Test 14   Adjectives and adverbs

Test 14.1
1 ~~happily~~ happy   2 ~~tiring~~ tired   3 ~~so good as~~ as good as
4 ~~better team B~~ better than team B   5 ~~well~~ good   6 ~~the more
successful~~ the most successful   7 ~~the larger~~ the largest

Test 14.2
1 the biggest   2 bigger than   3 as small as   4 better than
5 the best (as good as)   6 more difficult than   7 the most expensive
8 as expensive as   9 worse than (as bad as)   10 the worst

Test 14.3
1 slowly   2 hard   3 well   4 as/as   5 the best   6 cheaper than

Test 15   Linking words

Test 15.1
1 as well as   2 as well   3 so   4 because   5 Despite   6 Although

Test 15.2
1 the snow, I arrived at work on time.
2 analysts think that gold is a good investment, others disagree.
3 put in a more expensive bid, we won the contract.
4 conference, I made a lot of useful contacts.

Test 15.3
1 for   2 so that   3 to   4 for   5 in order to   6 so that

Test 15.4
1 to have lunch.   2 vacation for a rest.   3 map so that I don't get lost.

Test 16   Verb/Adjective + preposition

Test 16.1
1 for   2 with   3 on   4 in   5 to   6 to   7 for   8 in   9 with
10 on   11 for   12 on   13 to   14 in   15 with

Test 16.2
1 to   2 for   3 to   4 to   5 with   6 of   7 about   8 for   9 with
10 in   11 for   12 of   13 of   14 in   15 for   16 from

Test 17   Prepositional phrases

Test 17.1

1 out of   2 for   3 on   4 in   5 in   6 on   7 on   8 At   9 on
10 under   11 by   12 up

Test 17.2

1 ~~target~~   2 ~~date~~   3 ~~budget~~   4 ~~stock~~   5 ~~vacation~~   6 ~~cash~~

Test 17.3

1 in person   2 on strike   3 at short notice   4 on hold   5 by law
6 in writing

Test 18   Phrasal verbs

Test 18.1

1 out   2 over   3 out   4 down   5 up   6 up   7 down   8 up
9 down   10 up

Test 18.2

1 looks after   2 deal with   3 looked through   4 do without
5 got over   6 get back to

Test 18.3

1 keep up with   2 drop in on   3 run out of   4 get on with
5 cut down on   6 move on to

Index

M

make + object + infinitive without to p74D
many
    in questions or negatives p90D
    many or **a lot of/lots of** p90D
    with countable nouns p86C, p90D
as a matter of fact p114C
may (modal verb) u23, u25
    future probability p36D
    requests/permission p54C
    uncertainty p58D
might (modal verb) u23
    future probability p36D
    in reported speech p78B
    uncertainty p58D
mine (possessive pronoun) p98A
modal verbs u23, u24, u25, u26
    ability u23, p60A
    advice p56E
    certainty p58A
    deduction p58B
    expectation p58C
    future probability p36D
    in conditional clauses p66D
    in questions u15, p54A
    introduction to … p54A
    obligation and necessity u24, p60B
    opinions p56E, p60C
    permission p54C
    prohibition p56D
    requests u23
    suggestions p54D
    uncertainty p58D
more
    + adjectives p106B
    + nouns p108B
    more and more … (in comparisons) p106C
most
    + adjectives p106B
    the most + nouns p108B
much
    in questions or negatives p90D
    much or **a lot of** p90D
    with uncountable nouns p86C, p90D
must (modal verb) u23, u24
    deduction p58B
    in reported speech p78B
    must and **have to** p56A
    obligation p56A
    opinions and advice p56E
mustn't
    prohibition p56D
my (possessive adjective) p98A
myself (reflexive pronoun) p100A

N

necessity
    and modal verbs u24
negatives
    double negatives p92B, p100B
    with **anyone**, **anything** etc p100B
    with future p32A
    with **going to** p34A
    with modal verbs p54A
    with past continuous p18A
    with past simple p16A
    with present continuous p12A
    with present perfect p20A
    with present simple p10A
    with third conditional p68B
neither p92D
never
    with past perfect p28C
    with present perfect p22A
    with present simple p10C, p22A
no (in negatives) p92B
    no and **none of** p92B
No (interjection)
    different ways of saying **No** p40B
nobody/no one p100B
non-defining relative clauses p84D
none (of) p92B
nothing p100B
nouns u39, u40
    + singular or plural verb p88B
    countable nouns u39, u40
    ending in **-ing** p76A
    specific and general meanings p88A
    uncountable nouns u39, u40
now
    other words meaning p48B
nowhere p100B

O

object question p44A
objects
    with transitive verbs u33
obligation
    and modal verbs u24, p60B
of
    possession (**of mine**, **of yours** etc) p98C
on
    in prepositional phrases p122
    in time expressions p46C
    on, **in** and **at** p124A, B
on time or in time? p48C
opinions
    and modal verbs p56E, p60C
in order to/to + infinitive p116A
our (possessive adjective) p98A
ours (possessive pronoun) p98A
ourselves (reflexive pronoun) p100A
out of
    prepositional phrases p122